A Guide to the
Threefold Lotus Sutra

A Guide to the
THREEFOLD LOTUS SUTRA

by NIKKYO NIWANO

translated and adapted by
Eugene Langston

Tokyo · KOSEI PUBLISHING CO.

Reproduced on the front cover is a portion of the frontispiece
for the twentieth chapter of the Lotus Sutra painted in gold
and silver by Ryūsen Miyahara to be mounted with one of
the handwritten scrolls of the Threefold Lotus Sutra copied
by Nikkyō Niwano. Used by permission of Nikkyō Niwano.

This text originally appeared in Japanese in volume ten
of *Shinshaku Hokke-sambu-kyō* (A New Interpretation of the
Threefold Lotus Sutra) and later as the book *Hokke-sambu-
kyō Nyūmon* (A Guide to the Threefold Lotus Sutra).

Edited by Ralph Friedrich. Cover design by Nobu Miya-
zaki. Book design and typography by Rebecca M. Davis.
The text of this book is set in Monotype Baskerville with
hand-set Bodoni Bold for display.

First English edition, 1981
Ninth printing, 2007

Published by Kōsei Publishing Co., Kōsei Building, 2-7-1
Wada Suginami-ku, Tokyo 166-8535. Copyright © 1968,
1975, 1981 by Kōsei Publishing Co.; all rights reserved.
Printed in Japan.

LCC 82-118791   ISBN 978-4-333-01025-7

Contents

Preface

In recent years, as the crises facing humankind have become more numerous and more acute, interest in the Lotus Sutra has begun to increase. Thus it is that throughout the world people from various walks of life have come to regard this sutra as a valuable and practical spiritual guide for living in these troubled times.

Such high esteem for the Lotus Sutra—the last major sermons of Shakyamuni, the historical Buddha —is by no means solely a modern phenomenon. One of the earliest evidences of reverence for this sutra dates back almost seventeen centuries. In the mid-fourth century Kumarajiva (344–413) journeyed from Kucha, his homeland in Central Asia, to India for study and there he became learned in the teachings of Mahayana Buddhism. When he had completed his studies and was about to leave India on his mission of carrying the Buddha's teachings to other countries, his teacher, Suryasoma, recommended the Lotus Sutra to him, telling him to transmit it to the east and disseminate it there. In 401 Kumarajiva finally reached China, where he became an eminent translator of Buddhist scriptures. In the dozen years before his death he translated a number of Mahayana texts into Chinese, and the most important and best known is his elegant translation of the Lotus Sutra.

Following its transmission to China, Buddhism flourished there, producing many distinguished monks. Among all those monks, the great patriarch of the

T'ien-t'ai sect, Chih-i (538–97), who was said to be foremost in wisdom and virtue and was called "Little Shakyamuni," made an exhaustive study of all the Buddhist scriptures available to him. As a result, he concluded that the core of Shakyamuni Buddha's teaching is revealed in the Lotus Sutra, and thus in the latter half of his life Chih-i dedicated himself to studying, explaining, and disseminating this sutra.

It is not necessary to discuss here the history of Buddhism in Japan since its introduction in 538, for stating even a few facts will indicate the importance and influence of the Lotus Sutra in Japan. (1) Prince-Regent Shotoku (574–622) established his Seventeen-Article Constitution, Japan's first law code, based on the spirit of the Lotus Sutra. (2) After more than ten years of arduous discipline, the priest Saicho (767–822), who built the great temple Enryaku-ji on Mount Hiei, concluded that the highest form of religious practice was to disseminate the teachings of the Lotus Sutra through the doctrines of T'ien-t'ai Buddhism, and he founded the Japanese branch of that sect, Tendai. (3) The Tendai temple Enryaku-ji was the training ground for a number of outstanding priests, including Honen (1133–1212), founder of the Pure Land sect of Japanese Buddhism; Shinran (1173–1262), founder of the True Pure Land sect; Dogen (1200–1253), founder of the Soto sect of Zen Buddhism; and Nichiren (1222–82), founder of the sect that bears his name. Nichiren, in particular, revered the Lotus Sutra, and at the risk of his life he confidently protested to the government of the time that only belief in the Lotus Sutra could ensure the welfare and salvation of human society.

In the past fifteen years, through my work with the International Association for Religious Freedom, the

World Conference on Religion and Peace, and the Asian Conference on Religion and Peace, I have had frequent opportunities to talk with people of religion throughout the world. Whenever I have explained the teachings of the Lotus Sutra to them, almost invariably they have responded with deep sympathy and admiration, expressed in such words as: "That is indeed an excellent teaching for the salvation of human beings."

Such reactions are not limited to people of religion. For instance, the gifted Japanese naturalist and poet Kenji Miyazawa (1896–1933) is remembered for the masterly poem "Ame nimo makezu" (I Don't Bow to Rain), which reflects the teachings of the Lotus Sutra. In his will Miyazawa included the following instructions: "Print a thousand copies of the Japanese-language version of the Lotus Sutra and distribute them to my acquaintances and friends. At the end of the text in the sutra, write this message: 'The work of my whole life has been solely to bring this sutra into your hands out of the desire for you to come in contact with the teaching of the Buddha contained in this sutra and to enter the supreme Way to enlightenment.'" Miyazawa's words give us food for thought.

Why is the Lotus Sutra esteemed as the foremost and most wonderful teaching for humankind? Although we could find enough answers to this question to fill a book much larger than this one, in the final analysis all those answers can be condensed to just two points.

First, the Lotus Sutra reveals and explains the infinite possibilities open to human beings. People have an infinite capacity for degeneracy if left unawakened and unmindful of discipline, yet at the same time they have an infinite capacity for elevation if they live in accordance with spiritual truth. Today, people are simply falling ever downward. Unless we stop now and think and completely change our way of living, we will certainly destroy ourselves. The Lotus Sutra reveals and explains both the theory and the practice necessary for bringing about such a change. Thinking that there is no answer for human foolishness, we are likely to become deeply depressed. But if, through the Lotus Sutra, we come to the realization that it *is* possible to change human nature for the better, fresh hope and courage ceaselessly well up in our hearts and minds.

Second, the Lotus Sutra teaches that, since all nonliving and living things, including human beings, are manifestations of the great life-force of the universe, all of them are equal in terms of the fundamental value of their existence. A view of the world based on this thought naturally gives rise to a basic principle of living that can be stated as follows: "When human beings enjoy coexistence and mutual prosperity, respecting the life-force inherent in all existences, including themselves, and loving that life-force completely, great harmony will be achieved in this world. The ultimate happiness of human beings lies in such a state of mind." People have so far tended to consider all nonliving and living things except themselves as existences at their disposal and have exploited, consumed, and destroyed them at will, and one result of this kind of thinking has been the pollution of nature. If we do not correct our wrongdoing immediately, we cannot be saved. The Lotus Sutra not only makes us keenly aware of these facts but also serves as an always dependable guide to the new way of living necessary for us now and in the future.

Because the Lotus Sutra is such an important and

timely scripture, I have long cherished the hope that all people living today will come to know it. But I can easily imagine that people reading it for the first time may encounter certain difficulties, since the text was compiled in India some two thousand years ago and since it reflects the dramatic style common to oral literature and makes abundant use of highly symbolic expressions. For these reasons I decided to publish this guide to assist such readers.

Giving careful consideration to the relation among the thirty-two chapters of the Threefold Lotus Sutra— that is, the Lotus Sutra together with its opening and closing sutras, the Sutra of Innumerable Meanings and the Sutra of Meditation on the Bodhisattva Universal Virtue—this book not only outlines the contents of the sutra but also explains the major points of each chapter in easily understood language. If through this explanation more people become aware of the supreme Way to enlightenment, no matter how small their number, I shall be extremely happy.

Finally, I would like to remind readers that this book is only an outline of the Threefold Lotus Sutra: a simple guide to it. Because the sutra has long been appreciated as a work of great literary merit and because almost every word or phrase in it contains an important teaching, I would like to encourage readers to go on to the sutra itself. *The Threefold Lotus Sutra,* translated by Bunno Kato and others (Weatherhill/ Kosei, 1975), has been praised highly and is well worth reading. The many passages from the Threefold Lotus Sutra quoted or paraphrased in the present book are taken from that one. It is my sincere hope that my book *Buddhism for Today: A Modern Interpretation of the Threefold Lotus Sutra* (Weatherhill/Kosei, 1976) will also be of help.

PART ONE

The Sutra of Innumerable Meanings

Background

This first part of the Threefold Lotus Sutra is complete in itself, but at the same time it is a prologue to the voluminous Sutra of the Lotus Flower of the Wonderful Law that follows. As a prologue it sets the scene and prepares the way for what is to come. The principal elements of mature Mahayana teachings are stated in the Threefold Lotus Sutra, and while these teachings are developed from those of the historical Buddha, they must certainly come from a time later than his. But they are presented in the sutra, not without a certain reason and logic, as the final teachings of Shakyamuni Buddha in the form of sermons delivered just before his death, or entrance into nirvana.

At the opening of the Sutra of Innumerable Meanings we find Shakyamuni Buddha at Vulture Peak outside the City of Royal Palaces in the kingdom of Magadha—in the vicinity of what is now northeastern India. A vast multitude is assembled to do reverence to him and to hear him—numbers so vast, in fact, that we must suspend belief that they could indeed have been there and heard. These numbers are not to be taken literally but are meant to convey the intensity of the feeling of awe and the breathless attention of all the people, gods, demons, animals, informed and uninformed alike, and indeed of all creation, awaiting the message to follow. Heaven and earth make themselves fragrant and beautiful, music sounds, and flowers rain down by way of pleasing the Buddha and expressing joy in his being.

All the assembled creatures bow low in reverence and then sit quietly to listen. A number of bodhisattvas and disciples are spoken of by name, and one of them, the Bodhisattva Great Adornment, stands forth and addresses a hymn of praise to the Buddha.

An understanding of the doctrine of Innumerable Meanings is necessary before going on to the Lotus Sutra itself, which forms the bulk and essence of the Threefold Lotus Sutra, and so a reading of the Sutra of Innumerable Meanings settles the spirit and prepares the mind to receive what is to follow.

Since early times the term innumerable meanings of the title has had two senses. In the first sense the term is singular in that it refers to the real aspect of all things, of all the forms in the universe—in short, the true form that is at the heart of the apparent world visible to the naked eye. In other words, it is that world of true being that exists above the apparent world. The body or substance (the ultimate substance) of this real aspect, being infinite and not subject to measurement, is termed substance immeasurable.

In the second sense the term is plural in that it refers to all the countless appearances or phenomena of the visible, tangible world we live in, brought forth from the one true world that is the real aspect of things. These appearances or phenomena, as an extension or working of the real aspect at the root of everything, are infinite and immeasurably complex, and the extension or working is termed extension immeasurable and innumerable.

The teachings of the Buddha are founded upon perception of the real aspect of things, and so it is that from one single truth countless teachings emerge. Or stated the other way around, countless teachings resolve into, or return to, the one truth that is the real aspect of all.

The purpose of the Sutra of Innumerable Meanings, then, is the statement of these principles of the substance immeasurable and extension innumerable of the real aspect of the universe.

· 1 · Virtues

This opening chapter is the Bodhisattva Great Adornment's hymn in praise of the Buddha's perfect virtue and practice for the salvation of all living creatures.

First, the bodhisattva speaks of the meaning of the Law-body of the Buddha, the ultimate substance not apparent to the eye. The Buddha, while apparent there in a visible body, actually abides in the world of real aspect. Accordingly, he is not subject to the law of cause and effect that operates in the apparent world, is without distinction of self or other, and is at one with all and everything. This one abiding and unchanging root force, giving rise to all things in heaven and earth, is the ultimate substance, the virtue, the working of the Buddha.

Thus, from the beginning, the meaning of the ultimate substance of the Buddha is made clear. This is all perfectly evident to the Bodhisattva Great Adornment as a bodhisattva, however much his words to the ordinary person at first seem like something in a dream.

The Lotus Sutra proper may be thought of as the Buddha's simple teaching in parables and other forms to make the truth of these words "like something in a dream" comprehensible to ordinary people. Thus the Bodhisattva Great Adornment's hymn of praise at the opening of the Threefold Lotus Sutra becomes a statement to the assembled multitude of the great lesson to follow.

In the course of the bodhisattva's hymn in praise of the perfect virtue explicit in the Buddha's visible body, it becomes clear that such virtue was the result of his various longtime disciplines and practices. It also becomes clear that it was attained through the working of compassion and knowledge won, and through fearless exposition of the Law, and that all his virtues can be attributed to the accumulation of the good karma he acquired as an ordinary man.

The great proposition that the Buddha was once an ordinary man is one to make the everyday person stop and think. The truth hidden beneath these words is that the Buddha and all living creatures are equal beings. Moreover, the great thought pervading the whole of the Lotus Sutra is here stated without confusion: any living creature may through practice of the Way become a buddha. This is to be noted and remembered.

The bodhisattva's hymn continues as he praises the thirty-two signs of excellence of face and figure in

Shakyamuni's visible body, a celebration of the perfection of character expressed in a physical body. He observes that while the Buddha is provided with these signs of excellence, his being transcends both what has and does not have form. This we may take to mean that to those whose eyes see only the world of discrimination, the apparent world, the true nature is scarcely perceptible.

The true nature of all living beings is thus the same, though the expression of this true nature in bodily form may not be perfect. The Buddha had infinite virtue, and as that virtue appeared in his figure, all might joyfully venerate him, take refuge in him, honor him, and wholeheartedly bow in reverence before him. Whatever insight the Buddha gained, he was never satisfied, but through practice after practice of the Way, he attained his indescribably beautiful body. We cannot but be grateful for this appearance in a palpable body, though the real body was impalpable.

Two points are to be noted here. The first is that the forms of all living creatures are in their true nature the same. All life in its true nature is of the identical substance of the Buddha, but owing to insufficient practice of the Way and being filled with illusion, its appearance in visible bodies has an ugliness and a meagerness that bear no comparison with the Buddha. Yet if in their true nature they are of the identical substance of the Buddha, it is plain that any appearance in a visible form has the capacity to become one with the Buddha, and so on the one hand we may all have vast hope, but on the other we are made to stop and reflect.

This thought permeates the Threefold Lotus Sutra from first to last, and thus it is important, in preparing to read it, to fix clearly in mind the concepts of equality of the true nature and differentiation in appearances.

The second point is that the appearance of the Buddha in a palpable body is something for which we must all be truly grateful. Shakyamuni came into this world, and as a result of his practice after practice of the Way, he became possessed of that perfected character. Because of this living example of one who reached the state of buddhahood, we are taught that it is well if we but imitate him, and we are enabled to pursue a path toward buddhahood far easier than the painful course Shakyamuni trod. This is what we must be grateful for in his coming into this world.

Thus, as with great joy in our hearts we venerate the figure of Shakyamuni and accept and keep his teachings, we may merge into that ultimate substance of the Buddha that is not to be seen with the eyes. The words of the Bodhisattva Great Adornment thus suggest the right way to look upon the principal image of the faith.

• 2 • Preaching

The Bodhisattva Great Adornment now leads the assembled bodhisattvas in asking the Buddha what they should practice if they would undeviatingly attain enlightenment and come into the spiritual state of a buddha.

Shakyamuni's response is that the doctrine of Innumerable Meanings is the way that leads all to perfect enlightenment. He says that the beginning of comprehension of this doctrine is the perception that at the heart of all things in this world is a world that from the beginning of the universe has been unchanging, in which everything is equal and at peace. In the apparent world we see with our eyes. We may see large and small, appearing and disappearing, fixity and movement, things different and changing in every way. But it must be perceived that at the root of everything there is but one being, a world of one likeness, a void, to be precise, that everywhere is the same.

Having stated this truth of the void, the Buddha goes on to say that few perceive this truth, and that though in their real aspect all things are equal and in great concord, people see only the apparent forms before their eyes. They willfully calculate loss and gain, cultivate unwholesome thoughts, and act wrongfully, thereby bringing all manner of misery upon themselves, and they are never able to escape from the realm of error.

Bodhisattvas perceive all this, are stirred with compassion for all living creatures, and determine to rescue all people from their suffering. To this end, practice is essential to perceiving in all its depth the true and real aspect of all things. Thus the cause of human suffering is shown, and the mental attitude of the bodhisattva who would rescue mankind from suffering is made clear.

The Buddha then instructs the bodhisattvas to observe closely the distinctive shapes of apparent forms and their changing condition. It is essential to grasp the capacity, nature, and wants of the many, and just as their capacity, nature, and wants are infinitely various, so also must the manner of preaching and explaining the teaching to them be infinitely varied. But though the teaching be thus infinitely varied, yet it proceeds from the one truth. This one truth is totally undifferentiated, being formless, and therefore makes no differentiation. Thus the fundamental nondifferentiation at the heart of things is the one law that calls all things into being and moves them. This is called the real aspect of things.

Here, then, the term real aspect in its Buddhist sense is made clear. Ordinarily we understand this term to mean simply the real shape of things, but it is important at this point to remember this deeper sense of the term when we encounter it in such expressions as the "real aspect of existence."

As the Buddha continues his instruction, he explains that the compassion awakened in the mind of the bodhisattva who has perceived this truth underlying all things and made it part of himself will have uplifting results.

We need to observe here that the compassionate mind of the bodhisattva is not just a feeling of pity or sympathy but that it springs from the perception that all things are equal, that all people are equal, from the sense that others and oneself are all one.

The Bodhisattva Great Adornment again speaks, now to formulate a problem. The Buddha's teaching is so profound that ordinary people are not likely to grasp its full meaning. The bodhisattvas already understand without difficulty, but it is necessary to ask on behalf of those ordinary people in whose minds questions and doubts remain. During the Buddha's forty-odd years of teaching since becoming the Buddha, he has taught that all is void, that all things change and pass, and that nothing exists alone and of itself, and many have been rescued by the teaching.

But now the Buddha is preaching a new doctrine of Innumerable Meanings, and while one must think that this is basically no different from what has been taught before, still one must wonder and ask in what point it differs from the previous teaching to have him say that practice of the teaching of Innumerable Meanings will lead directly to supreme enlightenment.

In response the Buddha observes that after he attained enlightenment under the Bodhi tree and gazed upon all the world, the conclusion was inescapable that in their present stage living beings were not prepared to have that enlightenment explained to them. For this reason he sought to lead living beings to their salvation by preaching in a fashion appropriate to their circumstances, capacity, nature, and wants. Continuing in this fashion to preach within the bounds of their understanding, the Buddha has not yet had the occasion to reveal the innermost truth of the Law, and thus it is that forty-odd years have passed without complete explanation of the final unadorned truth.

Yet all that has been taught until now is founded on the truth. Like water, which everywhere is water and yet differs as does the water in a valley stream, a ditch, a pond, or the great sea, the teaching at the beginning, midway, and now has not been exactly the same. Although the words may appear the same, there has been increasing depth of meaning.

The truth that all the buddhas have taught is only one. The manner of explaining this one truth has been as varied as the many things men have sought in their minds. Again, the body, or ultimate substance, of buddhas is one. It changes into countless bodies, and each of these displays countless changes in its working. This is none other than the incomprehensible realm of the buddhas. It is a realm hardly to be known even to the bodhisattva verging on buddhahood, let alone to those with but the enlightenment attained through listening to the Buddha's teachings and practicing them or through independent practice without a teacher. It is a realm to be plumbed only upon attaining buddhahood, a realm to be known to none but buddhas. One who would gain this enlightenment of the buddha must go deeply, deeply into these Innumerable Meanings and master them.

In this sense Shakyamuni spoke, and today when we are taught of this body or substance of the buddha and its working, most of us probably get only a vague general idea. But no one can affirm that he understands clearly and fully. For to perceive clearly that substance of the Buddha which is the great life-force of the universe, and the boundlessness of its working, one must gain the knowledge and wisdom that are one with those of the Buddha. Then one is oneself a buddha. As the sutra has it, "Only a buddha together with a buddha can fathom it well."

But this does not mean that we should despair. At the time of the sermon that comes to us as the Sutra of Innumerable Meanings, not even Shariputra, that disciple first in wisdom, had attained enlightenment. And so it was that later, in the rather more easily understood Sutra of the Lotus Flower of the Wonderful Law, the Buddha patiently explained the Law in order that all living creatures might be brought to enlightenment. So it does not matter if one does not perfectly understand the Sutra of Innumerable Meanings. It is enough at this stage to outline in the mind, even if only faintly, the sense of the two terms the real aspect of this world and the ultimate substance of the Buddha and its working.

• 3 • The Ten Merits

The essence of the third chapter is the urgent advice to master and practice the teaching of the sutra for the spiritual merit to be gained from it, the good life it leads to, and the usefulness to mankind and the world that it makes possible.

The questioner, the Bodhisattva Great Adornment, asks where this teaching comes from, toward what purpose it tends, and where it dwells. The Buddha answers that its origin is none other than an outflow from the innermost mind of the buddhas; that its purpose is to stir the minds of all people to seek supreme enlightenment—that is, the wisdom of the buddhas; and that its dwelling place is in performing the practices of the bodhisattva.

The innermost mind of the buddhas is the will that all life shall fulfill itself after its nature. This is the fundamental will of the universe itself, and if only man would live in accord with this will his troubles would end. But man is captive of a willful self, lives after the dictates of that self he clings to, and thus brings suffering on himself.

We might think of the enlightenment of the buddhas as the perception of two realities. The first is the way in which always and everywhere the will of the only true being in this world, the great life-force of the universe, appears in unlimited operation (that is, innumerable meanings) in both inanimate and living things. The second is the way in which all things and all forms subsist and have their being after their nature.

Applied to man, this means seeing that the true way

to live is to live as one is. But the ordinary person so little understands how to live as one is that Shakyamuni resorted to all sorts of explanations of his teaching, depending upon the circumstances of his hearers. This adapted instruction has been described as tactful teaching.

Tactful teaching is an admirable and gratifying thing, but by virtue of its nature it brings up difficulties if, with changes in circumstances and position of the person, it happens that one fails to grasp the exact situation at any given time.

Thus it happens that the man of understanding is awakened to seek the supreme truth that applies to all men in all conditions. This is the awakening of the aspiration to buddhahood, and the object of the teaching of the Innumerable Meanings is to awaken this aspiration.

Now, in the response to the question where the teaching stays or abides, where it really is, where its true value is, we see that it is not in books or in the mind but in practice. Indeed, only in practice does the teaching come alive.

These three things—the origin of the teaching in the mind of the buddhas, its objective in stirring the aspiration to seek enlightenment, and practice—are elements of such paramount importance, pervading not only the Innumerable Meanings but all Mahayana teaching (the teaching of the Great Vehicle) as well, that it is essential here to grasp and keep them firmly in mind.

Returning to the text of the sutra itself, we next read the Buddha's explanation of the first of the ten merits:

"First, this sutra makes the unawakened bodhisattva aspire to buddhahood, makes a merciless one raise the mind of mercy, makes a homicidal one raise the mind of great compassion, makes a jealous one raise the mind of joy, makes an attached one raise the mind of detachment, makes a miserly one raise the mind of donation, makes an arrogant one raise the mind of keeping the commandments, makes an irascible one raise the mind of perseverance, makes an indolent one raise the mind of assiduity, makes a distracted one raise the mind of meditation, makes an ignorant one raise the mind of wisdom, makes one who lacks concern for saving others raise the mind of saving others, makes one who commits the ten evils raise the mind of the ten virtues, makes one who wishes for existence aspire to the mind of nonexistence, makes one who has an inclination toward apostasy build the mind of non-retrogression, makes one who commits defiled acts raise the mind of undefilement, and makes one who suffers from delusions raise the mind of detachment. Good sons! This is called the first inconceivable merit-power of this sutra."

The sense of this is clear enough, as is the sense of the remaining nine merits, and it is important for us to discern why there is such merit in the Sutra of Innumerable Meanings.

PART TWO

The Sutra of the Lotus Flower of the Wonderful Law

• 1 • Introductory

In this introductory chapter we pick up the thread that runs through the entire Lotus Sutra. It is the beginning, or prologue, of an exceedingly long sermon. But even though it is a prologue, its substance is not meager, for it suggests and prepares the way for the great truth about to be revealed.

For the person reading the Lotus Sutra for the first time, it is enough to feel that there is something impressive here, without appreciation of the suggestion and preparation. But for one who studies the sutra over and over and seeks to explain it to others, it becomes important to be aware of this suggestion and preparation and understand its meaning. It will not do to dismiss the chapter simply because it is where we pick up the thread.

Like the preceding Sutra of Innumerable Meanings, the Lotus Sutra opens with a statement of the setting and an enumeration of the principal personages in the multitude assembled to hear the Buddha speak. We are told that, having preached the Sutra of Innumerable Meanings, the Buddha entered a state of deep contemplation, at which the world and the universe itself expressed admiration and joy. The assembled multitude, which included monks and nuns as well as lay believers, Brahman deities, and beings and demons not even human, all placed their hands together in gratitude and gazed upon the Buddha, when suddenly there burst from the circle of white hair between his eyebrows a ray of light. This light illuminated every quarter of this world, all worlds beyond the heavens, and even the depths of the Avici hell of unremitting pain. Even distant future generations showed in the light as though they were real.

This extraordinary event struck the assembly with admiration, but it occurred only to the Bodhisattva Maitreya to wonder what it meant. Finding no answer in himself, he questioned that great one, that repository of wisdom, the Bodhisattva Manjushri. Maitreya's question is put once in prose, then repeated and elaborated at considerable length in verse.

Manjushri presents a lengthy answer, again first in prose, then in poetry, pointing out that in distant ages past there had been a buddha called Sun Moon Light Tathagata. (Tathagata is the highest epithet of a buddha.) Manjushri explains this buddha's teaching and proceeds, surprisingly enough, to say that after he was gone another and yet another to the number of twenty thousand buddhas appeared, all bearing the same name, Sun Moon Light Tathagata.

Next, Manjushri tells how the last of them taught the Innumerable Meanings for the benefit of mankind and then entered a state of deep contemplation, whereupon, as had just happened with the present Shakyamuni Buddha, a ray of light sprang from the circle of white hair between his eyebrows and illuminated countless worlds. "When the Buddha Sun Moon Light arose from his contemplation, he preached . . . the Lotus Flower of the Wonderful Law . . . [and] at midnight entered the nirvana of no remains."

Manjushri concludes that the present tathagata, Shakyamuni, is about to preach the Lotus Flower of the Wonderful Law for the salvation of all people and to make the world just and beautiful. With the poetic version of this the chapter closes.

As may be seen from this synopsis, the Lotus Sutra is in form a kind of drama in which all sorts of surpassingly extraordinary occurrences are treated. We may gather that the intent of the compilers of the sutra was to use familiar symbolic devices and drama to touch the spirits of hearers and to bring them bit by bit to an understanding of the truth set forth by Shakyamuni: a truth so deep that the people of the time could by no means grasp it completely. It is important to understand this.

The presence in the assembly of Brahman deities and even extrahuman demons and gods symbolizes the fact that the teaching of the Buddha is a truth not for humanity alone but for all creatures living and to come. This truth is ultimately one, regardless of the myriad forms that differing causes and conditions impose upon appearances. Accordingly, though religions teaching this truth may differ in form on account of ethnic and cultural differences, insofar as they are true religions they all go back in essence to the same truth. The fact that the deities of other religions assembled to listen to the teaching of the Buddha makes this clear.

The auspicious sign of the shaft of light springing from the brow of the Buddha and illuminating all the worlds of the universe means simply that true wisdom makes clear the true aspect of all things in the world. This wisdom is at the bottom of the Buddha's teaching, and this is what makes it rational and in no sense counter to the advanced science of our own time.

The fact that the light of this wisdom reaches all

worlds of the universe and future generations means that ultimate truth applies not only to earthly matters but also to the entire universe and not merely to the present but to the far distant future as well.

We may sum up the meaning of this auspicious sign by observing that true wisdom goes beyond time and space and makes clear the true aspect of all things. When this is understood, then the meaning of there having been twenty thousand buddhas Sun Moon Light in succession, all of whom preached the one Law, also becomes apparent. For if the truth be one, then all who have awakened to it will teach what at bottom is one and the same.

Shakyamuni, the historical Buddha, though he attained enlightenment through his own contemplation, claimed no originality for his teaching. He stated straightforwardly that "of yore I followed countless buddhas." This declaration stems not from modesty but from his conviction that the truth is always one.

• 2 • Tactfulness

This chapter, with chapter 16, "Revelation of the [Eternal] Life of the Tathagata," has long been regarded as the heart of the Lotus Sutra. It will be well to bear in mind the question of why this is so, but first we need to examine the plan of the chapter itself.

Near the beginning Shakyamuni concludes the meditation in which he has been engaged. Before anyone poses a question, he immediately begins to speak, addressing the disciple Shariputra. He explains that the wisdom of the buddhas is most profound, an awakening to the basic one truth of the universe. This basic truth is of such depth that ordinary people cannot understand it, and on this account, by using various ways of teaching within the capacity of their understanding, he has brought salvation to many. But the fact remains that they have not grasped the true meaning at the heart of the teaching. Having said this much, the Buddha suddenly stops, then resumes, again addressing Shariputra.

The reason no one has grasped the truth is that the perfected truth is such that only among buddhas can it be comprehended. The statement of this truth, known as the Ten Suchnesses, in briefest form is that everything in our world has its own appearance or visible aspect (form), its own character (nature), its own entity (embodiment), its own latent energy (potency), and its own working or functioning (function). The total of these four elements becomes a cause (primary cause), which, in contact with a condition (secondary cause), brings about myriad results (effect) and rewards (recompense)—that is, continuing effect. And although these nine elements seem different and multiple by appearance, all of them rest upon the universal truth and, in true substance, are from first to last a complete fundamental whole.

The statement in the sutra is swift and brief, and so we shall return to the point later. A difficult point of doctrine having thus been stated, the entire matter is reexplained in more memorable poetic form, embellished and further developed. The listeners, however, are puzzled at this new turn and do not know what to say.

Shariputra guesses the difficulty and begs Shakyamuni to go further and explain what he means by the tactful method of teaching: teaching in ways suitable to the occasion and to the people to be reached. This artful method is announced to be the kernel of the wisdom of the Buddha, and the great worth of tactfulness is praised.

Still, the listeners are all the more perplexed. While expecting to hear the supreme truth that the Buddha has seen, they are treated to words of praise for the everyday teaching of tact, and they are unable to see any connection.

Shariputra is not to be put off and is quite demanding as the Buddha three times declines to explain, on the grounds that what he has to say can only confuse and is thus better left unsaid.

Since, to begin with, the Buddha had of his own accord, with no prompting or questioning, begun to preach, we must suppose that this display of unwillingness had the purpose of creating in his hearers a suitable frame of mind to listen to what was to come. Then realizing, in response to Shariputra's pleading, that his hearers are ready, the Buddha is about to speak, when, in a body, five thousand of the assembly rise and depart. Shakyamuni simply watches, making no effort to stop them, and when all have left, he takes up his sermon again.

The continuation, first in prose, then in more memorable verse, can be summarized briefly. The aim and purpose for which buddhas have appeared on earth has been from first to last to awaken people to the truth that all men alike partake of the buddha-nature. Thus the object of the teachings of the buddhas is to lead all men alike to the state of buddhahood, but this does not mean that there are distinctions in the truth. The objective is always the same, although up to now Shakyamuni has turned to various ways of teaching as a matter of tact in order to achieve the objective.

The doctrine that all mankind could become buddhas had not been stated before, but the time had come to make it clear that whoever followed and practiced the teaching would become a buddha. This thought, though, is not to be taken to mean that all the earlier doctrine is useless. No matter how much it may appear that teachings adapted to need were only a temporary means of saving people close at hand, such teachings are part of the process leading to the wisdom of the buddhas, which is the true object. All the teachings are related to this supreme truth, and all ways are related to this supremely true Way.

One may look upon someone's standing before a pagoda saying a little prayer, or a child's drawing of a buddha on the ground, as things with no bearing on this, but actually even these are related to this supreme Way, the Way to buddhahood. One must by no means make light of the possible range of tactful means. We should remember that the tactful way as such is the truth.

The subject is developed at length, but in conclusion Shakyamuni states that whoever in simplicity and purity of heart gives attention to any of the multitude of tactful teachings, beginning with the explanation of the Law of Causation founded upon the supreme truth, that person is treading the Way to becoming a buddha. All will become bodhisattvas, will understand the truth, will rejoice exceedingly, and will become buddhas.

As we study this sutra, the first question that comes up is what in fact is meant by becoming a buddha. To attain buddhahood as a human being means to be an enlightened person, to attain the supreme knowledge that sees the real aspect of all things, to achieve perfection of character in which that knowledge is manifest in body and mind, to move in a state of perfect freedom, and to work for the salvation of all people.

We are bound to think that it must be almost impossible for ordinary people to attain such buddhahood, so remote is it from ourselves. But as is taught repeatedly after the Sutra of Innumerable Meanings, the real aspect of the universe is only a uniform void, and all being is alike in origin. In effect, then, this means that we ourselves are in ultimate substance uniform with the Buddha. And if we are uniform in ultimate substance, then it can only be that even in apparent form we are still uniform with that ultimate substance.

The general destiny of living things is evolution, which we may view as progress toward higher degrees of freedom. Those that are obedient to this destiny and strive toward a higher freedom evolve, while those that are thwarted by circumstances fail and devolve, or become extinct.

Yet people are different from all other living beings in having a spirit. It is in this spirit that their value lies, for otherwise in flesh and substance they are scarcely different from other animals. So it is truly human to walk the way of progress in quest of perfect freedom of this spirit. Or we might express it another way by saying that spiritual progress is mankind's noble destiny.

The goal of this spiritual progress is nothing other than the state of the buddhas. The ideal state for mankind, then, is the state of the buddhas that conveys supreme wisdom, perfect character, and spiritual freedom and leads to the salvation of all people. For this reason to aspire to become a buddha and to practice with the objective of the buddha state before one is no impossible dream. Nor is it the special action of chosen persons. It is the one Way, apart from all others, that mankind should pursue.

All unconsciously we ourselves may be walking that Way, for to study the teachings of the Buddha, to try to be better people, to place our hands together in gratitude before the Buddha, to do any small kindness, to drop a single good word—all are part of the Way to buddhahood. It may be that we have not noted that such little things are the Way to buddhahood, having thought of them only as means toward being better people, toward being happy, or toward enjoying a more livable society. But when we learn that the tactful way as such is the truth, our eyes are opened to the fact that we are walking in the Way of the buddhas.

This is an incomparable joy. One may think of himself as a person of no account. Then, hearing the teachings of the Buddha and seeking to put them into practice, he is likely to think that he is merely on the right road but that this is nothing much. But to realize that, far from being a person of no account, one is a worthy being who will become a buddha—that one is actually on that grand Way to becoming a buddha— is a thing for rejoicing and pride.

At this point one's natural course is to move quickly ahead, consciously and deliberately. Life takes on meaning, and one may boldly progress toward a new life. This is the great lesson of the chapter on tactfulness.

Another point of teaching in this chapter is the Ten Suchnesses, those of form, nature, embodiment, potency, function, primary cause, secondary cause, effect, recompense, and complete fundamental whole. I touched upon the general sense of this earlier, but we must see here that the last, the complete fundamental whole, in which root and branch are the same, is the uniform void. When manifest in apparent forms, the void assumes various forms. Each form has its nature, embodiment, potency, and function, and, with the unfailing operation of the laws of primary and secondary cause, effect and recompense follow. There is a great lesson here that we may draw about human life.

First, we human beings in our apparent forms have our own personalities, which is to say that each one of us has his own form, nature, embodiment, potency, and function. But since the origin from which all of them are derived is a uniform void and is always in a state of flux, it is possible to change our personalities.

We are accustomed to think of our personality as something we cannot help, but the lesson here is that this is not the case. Given a certain cause (primary cause) and condition (secondary cause), a suitable result (effect) and influence (recompense) follow, and since this is true, human nature may be changed.

Thus the heart of the human being has the inner capacity either to rise to the state of the buddha or to sink into hell. This idea is set forth in one of the commentaries by the T'ien-t'ai patriarch Chih-i (538–97) as the Three Thousand Realms in One Mind. A single human mind may become three thousand worlds.

The doctrine of the Three Thousand Realms in One Mind teaches us that we have the infinite possibility of moving both upward and downward. If we resolve firmly to practice the Buddha's teachings, we can go upward without fail. Secondly, this doctrine lets us realize clearly that in all the universe there is no individual existing apart from the whole and that all things are interconnected like the meshes of a net. Individual salvation alone is not true salvation.

Now, though we may think ourselves beyond change, if we realize that indeed we can change, that we can even become buddhas, then light may shine upon us and hope may well up in our breasts. With this we can only set ourselves to the task.

And, as we set ourselves to the task, if we also are awake to the teaching of the Ten Suchnesses, the way we look upon others changes. Above all, we become able to see the buddha-nature that underlies superficial personality in all people. With this our contempt for, and our passive acceptance of, the no-account and unreformable people around us may give rise to a sense of respect for them, because they too have the capacity to become buddhas. We hear much today of respect for humanity, but unless we mean by that what I have just described, it is not the real article. With a real sense of respect for humanity, when we see people floundering or in distress, a feeling wells up in us of wanting to help them to awaken to their real selves. We are filled with a sense of loving friendship and a desire to walk hand in hand along the true human way that is the Way to buddhahood. This is the spirit and mind of the bodhisattva.

To awaken this bodhisattva spirit in anyone, to

bring even one more person into the same Way, is to raise the level of humanity. I daresay this is the only way to build a truly ideal society. This is what we must see clearly in the teaching of the chapter on tactfulness.

• 3 • A Parable

Beginning with this chapter, the Lotus Sutra becomes much easier. The Buddha's teaching so far has been theoretical and philosophical, but here, with the introduction of a parable, there is an abrupt change to a style readily understood by ordinary people.

The second chapter of the sutra closed with Shakyamuni's statement that all would become buddhas, and now Shariputra, his face lighted with joy, rises to salute Shakyamuni and announce his ecstasy at the understanding just granted to him. First in prose, then in verse, he speaks of his own spiritual progress, which now, though not complete, is crowned with the certainty of his becoming a buddha himself and a teacher of bodhisattvas.

Shakyamuni then announces that in an age almost infinitely distant, yet seemingly near at hand, Shariputra will become a buddha whose name will be Flower Light Tathagata and whose domain will be the Undefiled, a land that is described as of itself bursting with abounding vitality and joy. This remarkable passage is repeated in poetry. Following the repetition, the assembled multitude rejoices at the prediction of Shariputra's perfect enlightenment, and the skies are filled with celestial robes offered in homage to the Buddha. Heavenly music and flowers come down.

A hymn of praise and thanksgiving follows, and then Shariputra again speaks to Shakyamuni. He states that his own doubts have been dispelled but that there are twelve hundred others at various stages of discipline and training who are perplexed by Shakyamuni's abrupt revelation of the new message about tactful teaching.

This announcement from Shariputra is the point of departure for the parable that is the body of the chapter.

It is necessary at this point to introduce one or two terms that appear in the following discussion. In the progress toward buddhahood, which is the fourth of the four holy stages, the first is that of the attender, the *shravaka*. *Shravaka* means a person who listens to the Buddha's teachings and exerts himself to attain the stage of enlightenment by practicing these teachings. *Pratyekabuddha* means a self-enlightened person who obtains emancipation for himself without any teacher. The common point in both of these stages is a lack of the wish and dedication to save other people. *Shravakas* and *pratyekabuddhas* do not teach and seek to save others. Their gain is viewed as merely personal salvation. In Mahayana teaching the two stages are often referred to as the two vehicles. The third stage is that of the bodhisattva—a Mahayana development—a being in the final stage before buddhahood or one who seeks enlightenment not only for himself but for all sentient beings.

Now Shariputra's joy stems directly from the buddhas, statement that all will become buddhas, but he is made even more joyous to have his own buddhahood specifically predicted. Until now he has been only a *shravaka,* clearly below the bodhisattva, and it had hardly occurred to him that he would reach that highest state of being, becoming a buddha himself.

In the chapter on tactfulness it is stated that "there is no other vehicle, but only the One Buddha-vehicle," which makes it plain that the way to buddhahood is but one and that there are no second or third vehicles. Then farther on, toward the end of the same chapter, Shakyamuni states that he is here to teach the bodhisattvas and that he has no *shravaka* disciples, which means that all the disciples are bodhisattvas and none are to be called *shravakas.* And then, at the end, he says, "Rejoice greatly in your hearts, knowing that you will become buddhas." And so, hearing this, those who had thought of themselves as mere students in the "high school" of the *shravakas* realized that their school was preparatory to the "college" of bodhisattvas, to borrow our contemporary language, and that while they had thought they were mere preparatory school students, they were in fact already in college. Moreover, since the college of bodhisattvas is the course to buddhahood, if only they continued to accumulate practice, they would become buddhas, and this truth they perceived clearly at the bottom of their souls. How could they not rejoice?

Hereupon Shariputra explains his gratitude but at the same time honestly confesses his previous inadequacy. In turn the Buddha confirms Shariputra's enlightenment and announces to him in particular that he is to become a buddha. This is the first of a number of predictions to *shravaka* disciples of their coming buddhahood, and the close disciples later all have their buddhahood predicted. In this sense the Lotus Sutra may be regarded as the Sutra of Prediction of Buddhahood—a major distinction—for it is the sutra that bestows upon all people the assurance that they may become buddhas.

Now, to return to the text, we read Shariputra's assertion first in prose, then in verse, that upon attaining the enlightenment of a buddha, he will preach the supreme doctrine and teach many. Shakyamuni's specific announcement of Shariputra's buddhahood, as indicated earlier, places it far, far in the future, but the prevailing feeling is one of its being near, as the realm of the Flower Light Tathagata is described in all its color and glory. Shariputra is content for himself, but he is worried over the twelve hundred others who are puzzled by the depth of the Buddha's teaching, and he pleads for a clearing up of this difficulty.

The World-honored One, Shakyamuni, then tells the parable of the burning house.

In a city in a certain country there was a great elder. His house was enormous but was provided with only a single narrow door. This house was terribly dilapidated, and suddenly one day a fire broke out and began to spread rapidly. The elder's numerous children were all inside. He begged them to come out, but they were all busy at their play. Though it seemed certain that they would be burned, they took no notice and had no urge to escape.

The elder thought for a moment. He was very strong and might load them all into some kind of box and bring them out at once. But then he thought that if he did this some might fall out and be burned. So he decided to warn them of the fearsomeness of the fire so that they might come out by themselves.

In a loud voice he called to them to come out at once to escape being burned alive, but the children merely glanced up and took no real notice.

The elder then remembered that his children all wanted carts, and so he called to them to come out at once because he had the goat carts, deer carts, and bullock carts that they were always wanting.

When the children heard this, they finally paid attention and fell all over each other in their rush to get out, and thus they were able to escape from the burning house. The elder was relieved at their safe delivery from harm, and as they began to ask for their carts, he gave each of them not the ordinary carts they wanted but carts splendidly decorated with precious things and drawn by great white bullocks.

Though the reader has perhaps already seen the meaning of this parable, we may explain it further by pointing out that the father-elder stands for the Buddha. The children are no other than ourselves, ordinary people, while the dilapidated house is our plain human society, and the fire is our physical and mental desire. This desire is the cause of human suffering. Because we are totally taken up with material things and our physical bodies and lose our spiritual liberty, we suffer. Moreover, foolish living creatures are not even aware that they have no spiritual liberty, and so on this account they do not understand that they are about to be consumed by the fires of their desire. Their minds are entirely taken up with daily life.

In order to relieve human misery, Shakyamuni presented various teachings. Human beings are of various kinds, and even among the seekers of the Way to salvation there are the *shravakas,* who have attended to the good teaching and are striving to dispel their delusion; the *pratyekabuddhas,* who by themselves in meditation and thought seek to open the Way; and the bodhisattvas, who as they seek supreme enlightenment at the same time give themselves to the salvation of all. When people find in the Buddha's teaching anything that exactly fits their own liking, they are unconsciously drawn into that teaching. This is the meaning in the parable of getting the children to come outside by themselves by offering each of them the cart he wanted.

So it is that although the teaching of the Buddha is at the end only the one Way to buddhahood, in the preparatory stages different artful and tactful means of teaching are employed. People then strive, each in accord with the individual lesson, to cultivate themselves, but as they practice and advance to higher levels, they discover that far ahead all the ways become one. This is the Way to buddhahood. The discovery that the way one has trod, which one had thought was only a second- or third-class road, actually turns out to be that supremely true Way is cause for great peace, hope, and joy. This is what is said when the children, who thought only that they would get goat carts, deer carts, and bullock carts, were all alike given the unexpected pleasure of a great white bullock cart, the best possible: the Way to buddhahood itself.

In reading this way, as if it were between the lines, one may find still other important lessons besides the principal one I have just outlined from this parable.

Another point to be noted, for example, is the way in which the elder first thought, because of his own great strength and power, to gather up the children bodily into some kind of box and drag them outside but then realized that this might be useless unless they could be made to come out by themselves.

This suggests how different it is to be saved by a power outside or by a power within oneself. For living creatures to be wordlessly dragged outside the world of suffering is to be saved by an outside power. But, engrossed in the pleasures and joys of the things before their very eyes, they may drop away and be lost, or, in the terms of the parable, the children may feel that playing inside the broad area of their burning house is to be preferred to the confining box prepared for their rescue. This is likely unless they themselves awaken. Moreover, once outside the burning house, they may still think the inside more amusing and go back.

At this point the elder, who stands for the Buddha, determined by some way to make them deliver themselves by their own strength. It does not matter what device is used to get them to run outside. Wanting a goat cart will do, or a deer cart, or a bullock cart. The point of value is that they come out of their own accord and will, for if they come out of their own accord and will, they will not go back again unless something unusual happens. Faith must be like this. If one only calls upon the gods or buddhas to deliver him, he is not likely to reach true salvation, because the very lack of desire and effort to make a better thing of his mind and heart, to correct his own conduct, will prevent him. Self-cultivation through personal practice of one's own will is the way salvation is achieved.

But the final goal of such practice is to do away with the little self, or ego, and, obedient to the universal truth, to become one with the great life-force of the universe. And so we must realize that this power within is not our own in the sense that lets us say, "*We* did this."

Faith that comes from the power within is no other than our own will and effort taking refuge in that absolute power that is the great life-force of the universe. So it is that the power within us is the power without and the power without, the power within. Otherwise there is no attainment of salvation. All this is suggested by the action of the elder in the parable.

Now we come to the matter of the single narrow door, the significance of which is that great revolution of the mind and heart that is the discarding of the egoistic self. The tremendous difficulty of this, so far as ordinary people are concerned, is symbolized by this narrow door.

Discarding the self, or egoism, occurs in a number of stages. The first stage is awakening to the simple truth, or principle, that human suffering is brought about by the collection of greeds and wants—desires— that make up the self. The realization of this alone represents a substantial step away from the self, but this is not enough if there is no awareness of the truth of what the self may give rise to.

At the second stage there must be the realization that in accordance with the Law of Causation all that we so urgently want and are attached to is a temporary appearance brought about by a concurrence of primary and secondary causes. Further, it must be seen that in accordance with the Law of the Twelve Causes the origin of those desires is ignorance, a basic misapprehension that the flesh is oneself.

When one perceives these laws, it becomes clear that the self to which one has clung is in fact something that has no real substance, and as a result one is automatically removed from self-centered thinking.

Then, with further practice, one may perceive the truth that all beings in this universe are at bottom void and identical, and with this realization one may fully taste the sense of unity that all are brothers, that all equally partake of the great life-force of the universe. When one has come this far, the self vanishes.

One of the most admirable and best known passages in the entire Buddhist canon is in this chapter.

> Now this triple world
> All is my domain;
> The living beings in it
> All are my sons.
> But now this place
> Abounds with distresses;
> And I alone
> Am able to save and protect them.

The universe is the Buddha's, all things, all people, are his sons, and he alone can deliver them from their pain and distress. But this is neither assertion of personal ownership of the universe nor boasting that he alone can save. What the Buddha is saying here is that there is no deliverance without casting away the self and merging with the Buddha.

If we can really cast away our selves, we may find in ourselves the great life-force of the universe that lives in all things. Then if we can gaze upon the life-force in ourselves that lives throughout the universe, our mind can in an instant go anywhere throughout that universe, and thus we may grasp the sense of what it means for the universe to be ours.

It is in this way that the mind becomes truly free. We are not hindered by anything, and, acting as we will, we are always in harmony with the truth, and our acts give life to ourselves and all people.

When the universe is ours, all the life that dwells in it is part of ourselves, and all things that have life are our children, our brothers or sisters. Thus, as a parent or brother or sister, we give ourselves to serve that life. This is the great, the true, compassion. It is none other than buddhahood itself.

These, then, are some of the lessons that are merely suggested in this chapter. The reason for their being only suggested is that those in attendance when the teaching was delivered could not understand, however clearly the lesson was put. This is why Shakyamuni then patiently continued his very long sermon. He knew that through his sowing seeds of impression by suggestion, at some time later sprouting would occur, and so he proceeded.

•4• Faith Discernment

Discernment, the second element of the title of this chapter, refers to understanding in the sense of rational thinking and decision in the mind that a thing is true, while faith, the first element, refers to the fixing of that understanding upon the mind, a condition of certainty in the truth of what has been understood.

We are accustomed to think it enough for ordinary

purposes of daily life to understand academic or technical information and to put it to right use, which is to say in conformity with theory, but that alone is not enough for the smooth functioning of our lives, since faith is essential.

A convenient example is the multiplication table we use every day. We need not stop to think each time we calculate—for example, why eight nines are seventy-two. The understanding of the tables we were taught as grade-school students becomes an embedded faith in the fact, and so we calculate smoothly, reciting with certainty the words seven nines are sixty-three, eight nines are seventy-two, and so on. With any truth, with any fact, this is enough, and indeed it is indispensable.

When we come to the teachings of religion, such faith is absolutely essential. Buddhism is a teaching fully in conformity with contemporary science, and so at the outset understanding is important, but this alone is insufficient. Through deepening of that understanding, a powerful feeling is born, a joy wells up in our being, and we achieve the soul's salvation as we come to feel at the bottom of our hearts the certainty of the teaching. This state of mind is one of belief, of faith. However rational the teachings of Buddhism are, unless we have faith and belief in them, their true worth does not become clear.

Now, returning to the text itself, we find at the opening of the present chapter that four other disciples have, like Shariputra, attained full faith and discernment through hearing the parable in the preceding chapter. These four are Subhuti, Maha-Katyayana, Maha-Kashyapa, and Maha-Maudgalyayana. They have all come to full faith in, and discernment of, the lesson taught by implication in the chapter on tactfulness. The lesson is that all people alike are provided with the buddha-nature; that anyone, no matter who, may become a buddha; and that while the Buddha employs all kinds of tactful and artful means in explaining the teachings, those tactful teachings are all for the sole purpose of helping people discover their own buddha-nature and awaken to the buddha's state of mind.

Here the four disciples declare the awakening in their minds and hearts, and they then go on to explain in the presence of the Buddha precisely how they awakened. This is of importance because when one recounts a spiritual experience to others, the experience itself becomes firmer and more nearly perfect. Maha-Kashyapa stands as spokesman for the four and tells of their experience in one of the flowers of the Lotus Sutra, the parable of the poor son.

There was once a boy who left home and became a wanderer. Until he was fifty, he wandered from place to place, working as a poor hired hand, but as the shadow of age crept upon him, instinctively and in spite of himself he found his way to his father's place.

His father had grieved over the loss of his only son and had gone everywhere in search of him but, never finding him, at last had settled in a certain town. He was a man of exceedingly great wealth, and he built in this town a magnificent mansion.

The son at the end of his wanderings happened upon this place and passed before his father's house. Thinking to get some work here, he looked in and saw a person so magnificent that he seemed to be a king, attended by crowds of servants in the midst of gorgeous surroundings. He was overcome with fear, for this surely was no house to employ a man like him, and, alarmed at the thought of being seized and put to work if he loitered, he started away to find some poor place more suited to him.

Meanwhile, his father, who never for a moment had forgotten that face, had at once recognized the poor man before his gate as his son and immediately sent servants to bring him in. But the son, who had no idea of what was in his father's mind, feared that he might be killed, and he fainted as he tried to break away from the servants sent for him.

Seeing all this, the father told the servants not to force the poor man to come. A few days later he sent two servants in shabby clothes to the wretched hut where his son now was, having instructed them to allure him with the offer of twice the usual wage for the lowly work of removing a heap of filth. By this means they were able to bring him back to his father's house. The rich man himself dressed in poor clothes and was thus able to calm his son's fears and to approach him, talk with him, and encourage him. After a time he told him he wished to treat him as his own son.

The poor son, for his part, rejoiced in such treatment but could never shake the feeling that he was an underling. The father bit by bit gave him more and more important work to do until at last he made him manager of all his property. The poor son worked faithfully and discharged his duties beautifully, but still he could not throw off the consciousness of his lowliness.

In time the poor son's feeling of inferiority lessened, and the father, in anticipation of his death, called together the king and the principal citizens to announce that the man he had taken in was actually his son and that all his property belonged to this son. It was only now that the poor son realized that this very rich man was actually his father, and his joy was unbounded as he learned that his father's vast properties were his own.

So runs the parable. The rich man of the story is, of course, the Buddha, while the wandering son is all living beings. Though all of us are children of the Buddha, we are not aware of our lofty birth, and so of our own accord we turn our backs on the Way of the Buddha and go out to wander in a world of sufferings. But the bond of blood between parent and child is not to be denied, and though we may roam the world in ignorance that we are children of the Buddha, in ignorance of our buddha-nature, at some stage we instinctively draw near the abode of the Buddha. This can only be an affirmation of the true nature of the human being, and it is ineffably precious.

Though living beings may not know that the Buddha, before whose gate they stand, is their father, the Buddha clearly recognizes his own. This is a point of profound meaning. We ourselves may be unaware that the Eternal Buddha that is the great life-force of the universe is ever fully present within and about our minds and bodies, but that true Buddha awaits our notice. Truth is ever waiting to be known.

On this account Shakyamuni, the World-honored One, appeared in the world to make it known that the Eternal Buddha and humanity are one substance. But because of the great depth of that teaching, people think themselves too lowly ever to approach that other realm and instead grow frightened and flee from the gate of the teaching.

And so, as a tactful means, Shakyamuni employed servants who looked like ordinary people—two kinds of servants who from work in the Buddha's house were firm in mind, that is to say, *shravakas* and *pratyekabud-*

dhas—with the thought that if people like these went, the minds of the lowly might be moved to join them and become servants in the house. In other words, the Buddha never abandons humanity but seeks in one way or another to bring all to see for themselves their buddha-nature and to awaken of themselves to it.

In the parable the poor son was first put to work clearing away filth, which is to say that he was made to practice clearing his mind of illusions. Through such practice he became familiar with the Buddha's ways in preparation for being made his son, for being brought to that state in which he might have the same awakening as the Buddha. But the son clung to his own lowly state in the belief that the enlightenment of the Buddha had nothing to do with him, being of a different order altogether, and this is why he had to continue long in practice.

This is an important lesson not to be overlooked: that the capacity to awaken to the state of the Buddha is only gained by long-continued practice. Thus it is that one becomes well grounded in the teaching and gradually achieves mental freedom, whereupon the keys are turned over and all the stores of the teaching are at hand.

Yet even so, and even though engaged in the important work of transmitting to others the teaching of the Buddha, there is no realization of being actually the Buddha's son, no awareness of the true nature that is identical in substance with the Buddha. Rather, one sees the Buddha as master, oneself as servant, with a clear line between.

Now the Buddha, in preaching the Lotus Sutra before entering nirvana, set forth the great truth that the Buddha and humanity are not strangers. Nor is their relation that of controller and controlled. Rather it is essentially the one-substance relation of parent and child, and so anyone may succeed to all the riches of the Buddha. Anyone may attain buddhahood. Any being may understand the truth of the Buddha's teaching. The great joy of having the untold riches of the Buddha's enlightenment is accessible to all.

The spirit of the lesson in the parable may be stated in a few words. Every wandering, erring human being should set aside base thinking and awaken to the truth that he is a son of the Buddha. All people must awaken to the worth of their true nature.

With such self-awareness one becomes incapable of acting basely. Even though physical and mental desire may beset one as before, he is not upset or pained thereby. Even though desire beset him as before, he may of his own accord turn it in the right direction. This in itself is a great salvation.

• 5 • The Parable of the Herbs

The chapter opens with the Buddha's commendation of Maha-Kashyapa for relating the parable that formed the heart of the preceding chapter on faith discernment—a parable that aptly explained the true merit of the tathagata, one who has earned the highest epithet of a buddha. The Buddha then proceeds, in the parable of the herbs, to explain the relationship between the teaching and receptive humanity.

He affirms Maha-Kashyapa's statement that the tathagata has infinite merit, full knowledge of the truth, and full freedom in presenting it, so that it serves all men equally, leading them at last to perfect knowledge of the Buddha. By way of illustrating this, the Buddha describes the plants that grow over the earth, of which there is every size, shape, and description, all alike thirsting for moisture-giving rain. A great cloud covers the sky, and rain falls. The rain falls everywhere upon the earth, and all the plants are wet evenly and abundantly. Herbs, grasses, bushes, saplings, and great trees all take in the life-giving moisture and grow. And though the rain falls upon all alike, each grows, takes its shape, blossoms, and bears fruit according to its own nature.

Just so, the Buddha tells Maha-Kashyapa, is the tathagata. He is the cloud covering the sky. His teaching is the rain falling everywhere upon the earth, and humanity and all living beings are the infinite variety of vegetation.

The tathagata's teaching is the truth of the universe. This truth at root is but one, which is void. This teaching, like the moisture-giving rain, is of but one form, one taste. But all men differ in their make-up and nature, in birth and upbringing, in health, in surroundings, in trade. These differences, despite the fact that all people are absolutely alike in their basic buddha-nature, give rise to differences in receptivity to the rain of truth.

But however great these differences in receptivity, all receive the rain of the truth suited to themselves, and all alike, according to their heaven-given nature, grow, flower, and bear fruit. A plant has no knowledge of whether it is superior, indifferent, or lowly; it merely grows after its given nature.

Man, in the eyes of the Buddha, is like a plant. What is one's place or position? What is one's value in the universe? Perhaps no man can really know. Only the Buddha can know. The Buddha rightly sees the place and state in which every man is and the shape of his spiritual being. And the Buddha further knows that one and all are absolutely equal in the springs of their being.

On the basis of this certain knowledge, the Buddha presents the teaching in a fashion suited to every individual, thus delivering all from the toils of life and setting everyone upon the right road of spiritual progress. Salvation appears to take various forms, but at root the teaching is only one, and it falls like the rain upon all alike. It is on this account that the form of teaching, of salvation, varies with the nature, character, and circumstances of each person, to the end that every person may be enabled to accept it. This is a supreme quality of the Buddha's Law.

The lesson of the parable is thus the formal variety and essential identity of Buddhist salvation, but we may also glean the lesson that right wisdom is awareness of the fundamental identity of mankind in the presence of apparent difference.

To lean entirely to awareness of the void that is this essential identity is to be like those Chinese "immortals" of old so remote from the world that they subsisted on air, and the attitude is scarcely suitable to real life. But it is equally wrong to be seized entirely by the infinite variety in apparent forms, for feelings of superiority and inferiority give rise to the snares of pride, arrogance, insulting haughtiness, envy, hatred, and conflict, while desire entails struggle and pain, and there is no hope for the salvation of human society.

Whatever differences there may be in superficial form, the true nature that is central to all people is, as such, one substance with the great life-force of the universe. Whoever has a firm grasp and awareness of this truth is enabled to live rightly, to make his own life and the lives of others truly meaningful. It is in this way that we may apply the lesson of this chapter to our lives today.

• 6 • Prediction

Just as Shariputra's buddhahood was predicted in chapter 3 of the sutra, in the present chapter Shakyamuni recognizes that four other disciples —Maha-Kashyapa, Maha-Maudgalyayana, Subhuti, and Maha-Katyayana—have achieved discernment of and faith in the Law, and here he foretells their buddhahood.

Prediction, as pointed out earlier, in the chapter on tactfulness, means assurance of attaining the enlightenment of a buddha and thus of attaining buddhahood at some future time.

But the prediction, or assurance, is conditional. As it is stated, the achievement of buddhahood may seem near at hand, but in fact it is to be attained only after long, long practice at an almost indefinitely distant time in the future. If we think about the meaning of this in contemporary terms, it is somewhat like being admitted to a fine school or university. The admission is essential and important, but admission papers are not a diploma. Study is an absolute requirement in learning, just as practice is essential in religion. We may see here, then, a somewhat different aspect of the power without and the power within ourselves, which was described indirectly and suggested in the parable in chapter 3.

• 7 • The Parable of the Magic City

The foregoing chapters have shown through parables the form and working of the Buddha and the Buddha's Law. This chapter and the next two treat of causal relations with the past, and they are further aids to those who may not yet understand.

Here Shakyamuni speaks of the close causal bond linking him with the disciples in the past, for the purpose of encouraging the disciples in their practice and affirming their attainment of buddhahood in a future life. The teaching here is that truth is eternal and unchanging and human life everlasting, so that ultimately all beings attain buddhahood.

At the opening of the chapter Shakyamuni speaks of a time ages and ages ago, so distant in the past that

the mind cannot grasp it, when there was a buddha
named the Universal Surpassing Wisdom Tathagata.
His attainment of enlightenment occupied a vast
period of time, but previously he had been a prince
and the father of sixteen sons, the eldest of whom was
named Wisdom Store. Long after he had left them to
become a monk in a distant land and had at last
attained perfect enlightenment after long practice,
Wisdom Store and his brothers learned of this attainment and determined to follow in his footsteps. Their
mothers and aunts were in tears to see them off, while
their grandfather the king and a retinue of ministers
and subjects went with them to the abode of the
Buddha Universal Surpassing Wisdom.

At this point in the sutra, the king in a passage of
verse reviews how the man who had been his son had
passed from ordinary humanity through years of
austerity and practice for the salvation of living beings
to the attainment of buddhahood. He declares the
homage of all people to this buddha and expresses the
joy they all feel in knowing that they may gain the
greatest happiness. At this, the sixteen princes join in
the hymn of praise and beg for instruction in the Law.

A long sequence of praises and entreaties follows,
after which the Tathagata Universal Surpassing
Wisdom presents a summary of the teaching, review-
ing the Law of the Twelve Causes. These are briefly
stated as well understood without further explanation.
A rather lengthy passage follows, describing events
ranging through vast time and space as the tathagata
is described as several times repeating the teaching
and freeing countless beings from error. In this long
interval the sixteen princes have become novices in
the practice of the teaching. The tathagata preaches

this selfsame Lotus Flower of the Wonderful Law for ages and ages without cease, and then he rests, absorbed in meditation. At this point the sixteen, now bodhisattva-novices, continue with the preaching. At length the tathagata again speaks, recounting how these sixteen have served past buddhas, practiced the Law, and brought the teaching of the Lotus Sutra to countless living beings, not in one life only but repeatedly as these countless living beings were reborn with the bodhisattvas, hearing their teaching and taking it firmly into their hearts in faith and understanding.

At the conclusion of this somewhat difficult passage we are again in the original setting of the sutra. But this is not at once apparent, since the Buddha, continuing the sermon of which the foregoing was of course a part, names the buddhas that the sixteen bodhisattva-novices have become and the quarters of their abodes in all nations in which they preach the Law. The sixteenth of these, now speaking, is Shakyamuni Buddha, who has attained perfect enlightenment in the *saha*-world—the world of suffering that is our own. The instruction and salvation of this *saha*-world is his lot. People to whom he has preached the Lotus Sutra in the past are the disciples and others now listening before him, and in the future there will be other believers—ourselves today—who by this same sutra may gain deliverance.

The sermon continues as Shakyamuni declares that the Tathagata is not always in this world in human form, for, having fully delivered his teaching, he will be elsewhere. But if many are firm in faith and understanding, aware of the truth of human equality, and steadfast in mind, he has presented for these the teaching of the Lotus Sutra when leaving this world. This is what he has taught in the past and what he is teaching now. There are no two ways, only the single, inner teaching of the Lotus Sutra. The tact of the Tathagata and the ways he employs to lead people into the one Way proceed from his deep understanding of the nature and capacity of living beings. Many people are the captives of their sensual desires, inviting suffering upon themselves, but he leads them to do away with their illusions and to gain peace of mind. The manner in which he does this he then makes clear by relating a parable, the fourth of the seven parables in the Lotus Sutra: the parable of the city in a vision.

In a certain place, far from human habitation and beset with wild beasts, there is a long, perilous, and difficult road leading to a place of rare treasure, and a large company of people are traveling this difficult road in an effort to reach that treasure. The leader of the band, a man of surpassing wisdom and shrewdness, knows the road in all its turnings to its destination.

Some in the party at length tire in body and determination, and, giving out along the way, they urge their leader to give up the long journey ahead and turn back. The leader is familiar enough with suitable occasions and ways of bringing pitiful humanity out of danger. He knows that if he can just get them to hold out a little longer, they will not give up pursuit of the great treasure they can gain with only a little more effort. And so he produces out of the strength of his resources a phantom city, placed a little beyond the halfway mark on their journey. He tells his followers to fear no more, that there is now no turning back, for they may all enter the city before them and rest securely.

So they all enter the phantom city rejoicing and make themselves comfortable. Then, when the leader sees that they are all rested and refreshed, he causes the city to disappear. And, urging the company on to the place of treasure now close at hand, he reveals to them that the city where they were was but a temporary thing, a device he had used to give them rest and restore their spirits. Thus encouraged, they are safely brought to their destination.

The chapter closes with a summary of its contents, highly condensed in memorable verse.

As in the parables of the burning house and the wandering son, the meaning here is the twofold principle of the single vehicle of the Buddha's teaching and the truth of tactful means. But this is not a mere repetition, for there is a new shade of meaning: the feeling of a new departure, a suggestion of the inspiration that comes into our lives from creation.

The long, hard road here is the journey of our lives, and on this journey we encounter all sorts of hardships and pain. We all strive to overcome these, but things seldom go as we want, and many of us, in the ordinary course of things, give up.

Many a good man has fallen into the defeatist way of thinking that however much he struggles he gets nowhere and that his best course is in one way or another to slip out of difficulties and get what pleasure he can out of life. In short, he gives up the effort to progress and escapes into an easy attitude toward life. On the other hand there is the man of little moral uneasiness—the man who readily falls into evil ways as he seeks in whatever he does to take the short way with little thought for the consequences.

People at both of these extremes miss the true significance of life, for, as explained in some detail earlier, constant progress is the natural course of living things. It is the right and true way for man to live. To be defeated by the pains of human life, to forget this natural and true way to live, to stop midway or to turn back, is to cast away the worth one has as a human being.

The Buddha taught a single attitude of mind, saying to mankind, so to speak, "Wait! If you only do this, you may lead a peaceful life with neither suffering nor anguish. The apparent forms before your eyes are just appearances that pass. Do not be deceived, and you may always be at peace." In so many words, we are told to go beyond appearances. Thus the aspiration may arise in any mind that if one sees things fully in this way, it becomes possible to lead a peaceful life. This is the meaning of the instruction given by the leader in the parable as he produces the great city ahead and directs the company in his charge to go there and rest.

But while his followers rest he causes the city to vanish and urges them on to the ultimate ideal of human life that lies ahead. The people are at first surprised and confused, but they recover quickly and set out once again.

Human life in the true sense means creative and harmonious living. We are instructed to go beyond appearances if we would escape human suffering and reach a state of peacefulness of mind, but this state is only a stage on the way to enlightenment. For though as practitioners of the Way of the Buddha we may deliver ourselves from suffering, great numbers of people in the world remain trapped in suffering. To pass these people by and reach a realm of ease for ourselves alone is again a kind of escape, an arrogant selfishness. This is in no sense enlightenment. To strive in the midst of suffering humanity for the well-being of all is to live a truly human life. Thus we must do away with any feeling of temporary ease and contentment, leave the phantom city, and set out again upon a road of new toil.

But though this toilsome road may seem the self-same road we have struggled along thus far, in fact it is toil of quite another dimension. And the worth of this toil is immeasurably greater, for it is the bodhisattva's toil for the happiness and well-being of people. When we perceive that as we toil and create things and ideas, our lives take on meaning, our hearts are lifted to that state of mind in which toil is pleasure.

Thus if each of us in the journey of life strives always after his nature, talent, and occupation to create those things that make for the happiness and well-being of others as well as himself, of the entire world, then that work of creation will most certainly make for a greater harmony. And such creation and the resulting state of harmony are the ultimate human ideal, a treasure of the highest order.

The chapter of the parable of the magic city is filled with important lessons, a basic one being the Law of the Twelve Causes, the twelvefold chain of causation. Four lines, first pronounced by the assembled Brahma heavenly kings, also occur here, and to this day they form the concluding words of services in virtually every sect of Buddhism:

> May this merit
> Extend to all
> That we with all the living
> May together accomplish the Buddha-way!

•8• The Five Hundred Disciples Receive the Prediction of Their Destiny

The theme of this chapter is the assurance given Purna and many of the other close disciples that they will surely attain to the state of buddhas. The declaration to Purna is given first in prose, then in verse, as the story is told of his past accumulation of merit, his future glory as Law Radiance, and the perfection of his abode at that time. At the conclusion of this, twelve hundred *arhats* standing there silently wish to be assured in the same way, and the Buddha, reading their minds, proceeds to name first Ajnata-Kaundinya, who at a time far in the future will become a buddha whose title will be Universal Light Tathagata. Five hundred others, some of whom also are called by name, are also assured that they will all attain perfect enlightenment and have the same title, Universal Light. The meaning here is that any hearer of the teaching who truly strives for enlightenment will finally reach this same state. The sequence of assurances is repeated in verse, and at the close of this verse passage Maha-Kashyapa is given the command,

> To these, who are not in this assembly,
> Do you proclaim my words.

It will be remembered that in the chapter on tactfulness, as the Buddha was about to speak, five thousand of the old disciples rose in a body and left, and it is to these that he now refers. The meaning of this is that once anyone has heard the teaching of the Buddha, a bond is formed, and even though one who has heard may turn away, the bond is never broken. At some time there is a remembrance and return to the path of the Buddha and eventual attainment of enlightenment. Similarly, we ourselves today become disciples of the Buddha and learn the teaching of the Lotus Sutra, and if we practice it, we also will become Universal Light Tathagatas.

As the name clearly indicates, such a one is a presence casting light everywhere in the world. In the same chapter the Buddha declares that all these tathagatas "in turn shall predict," by which is meant simply that in terms of ourselves one tells another, this other another, ever in turn, and we who learn and practice the teachings of the Buddha will sometime predict the enlightenment of another. We have the duty to make this prediction. Thus, gradually, Universal Light Tathagatas multiply, and our world at length will become a pure land filled with light.

This is the meaning we may read from the superb foretelling that is the theme of this chapter. Indeed, I daresay this is the meaning we must read.

The disciples who directly receive the Buddha's assurances are overjoyed, and they stand in gratitude before him, reproving themselves for the pride and satisfaction they had until then felt in their wisdom. They confess their condition with a parable, which is related by Ajnata-Kaundinya, first in prose, then in verse. This is the fifth parable: the parable of the gem in the robe.

A certain poor man went to see a good friend. This friend entertained him with food and wine with the result that he got quite drunk and fell asleep. Just then the friend was called away on business, but, hating to wake the sleeping poor man, he thought what he might do for him, and he sewed a priceless jewel into the lining of his clothes. He then went away on his business.

When the sleeper awoke and found his friend gone, not to return for a long time, he also left and resumed his wretched life of wandering. He was in great need of food and clothing and was content with whatever small amount he could earn.

A long time passed, and one day the poor man, still unaware of the jewel, met his old friend on the road. The friend looked at the poor man's pitiful condition and said, "How could you be so stupid? Look at yourself! I sewed a precious stone into the lining of your clothes just so you would be able to live comfortably." Then he reached over and took the jewel from the lining of the filthy collar and said, "See? Sell this and buy whatever you need. Why should you be in want?"

In this parable Ajnata-Kaundinya is saying that the Buddha is like this good friend, that when he was still a bodhisattva he had told his followers that they all alike had the same buddha-nature—the priceless jewel of the parable—and that through practice they might all gain the enlightenment of the Buddha. But their minds had been plunged in sleep, and they failed to grasp the true meaning. In getting rid of physical and mental desire, they had thought they were enlightened, but aspiration after the perfect enlightenment of the Buddha remained. Somehow they sensed there was something more, and now the World-honored One had awakened them. Now they knew that they themselves were bodhisattvas. Now, striving for mankind in their practice as bodhisattvas, they knew that ultimately they would become buddhas. Filled with joy at so great a good, they declare their gratitude from the heart. The chapter closes with the poetic summary of this passage and its thought.

The buddha-nature is the capacity to become a buddha, or, to put this in ordinary terms, it is the capacity to become a person of perfect wisdom and virtue. If we ask how we may be sure that everyone has this capacity, we may answer that all people are of the ultimate substance, the absolutely identical and everlasting life that is animated by the great life-force of the universe. Thus, basically speaking, the buddha-nature may also be termed the Eternal Buddha.

Though all of us have the buddha-nature in this sense, we are often not able to see it ourselves. The reason for this is that we are accustomed to think that our selves are the little bodies and minds working away for our daily needs and running hither and thither in pursuit of our wants. The poor man of the parable is the very picture of us ordinary people. His rich friend, like the Eternal Buddha bestowing the buddha-nature upon every mortal, has given him a precious stone, but he does not realize that he has it, and we, like him, seek only the satisfaction of our wants and do not notice the precious thing we have. And so we are the more lost as we go on and on in the complications of our lives.

But the Buddha who appeared in this world as Shakyamuni taught that all mankind alike have the buddha-nature—the priceless jewel in the lining of the poor man's clothes in the parable—and this teaching stirs our awareness. The instant we gain this awareness, our minds expand, brighten, and become free, and we gain great confidence in human life.

In summary, then, the parable states the truth that really we are already delivered. Our ultimate substance is that free life that is one with the great life-force of the universe. Because we do not know this, we are caught in the toils of life. But deliverance is not hard. We need only to make the discovery, to awaken to the fact that our ultimate substance is the buddha-nature, to see that in our beginning in this way we are delivered.

•9• Prediction of the Destiny of Arhats, Training and Trained

Now, after so great a number of disciples as the five hundred had received their predictions, Rahula, Shakyamuni's only son, and Ananda, his cousin, both of whom were numbered among the ten great disciples, felt outcast and began to wonder why they, among so many, should not also be directly designated. But when they went before the Buddha and asked to be included, the Buddha then and there gave them their prediction and at the same time predicted buddhahood for a great number of the training and the trained, by which is meant those who as practitioners were still engaged in study or as *shravakas* had completed their study. This in brief, is the content of this short chapter, but there are two important lessons to be learned from this simple material.

The first lesson lies in the prediction given to those who still were training, those practitioners who were learning by doing under guidance. Though this may seem strange, careful reflection makes it plain that there is nothing at all strange in this, for since all people alike are endowed with the buddha-nature, if that buddha-nature is manifest and fully recognized, then all who perceive their buddha-nature may become buddhas.

The second lesson involves the question of why prediction for Rahula and Ananda among the ten great disciples was deferred and was then delivered with the prediction for *shravakas* still engaged in study.

Here we need to try to see into the thinking of Shakyamuni. Rahula was the son of his flesh, and Ananda was his own cousin. For twenty years or more both had been constantly at his side and had served him, and so both were closest to Shakyamuni in his person, a fact that in itself may have been a hindrance to their practice. So we may think that on this account Shakyamuni purposely delayed in order to make this point clear to all.

In the case of Ananda, he was always at hand, preparing Shakyamuni's food, assisting him at his bath, and seeing to his person, and so his perception of Shakyamuni's greatness as the Buddha and of the loftiness of his teaching was mingled with that of Shakyamuni as a human being in the flesh. His devotion thus lacked the purity characteristic of that of the other disciples.

In the case of Rahula, we may have the combination of a son's incapacity to find in a father, however great, the cause for respect that people at greater distance feel, mingled with a certain readiness to take advantage of being the son of such a person.

Seeing all this from our own point of view, we may know how very difficult it is to influence those closest to us—our wives or husbands, our children or parents.

We may seek to lead with words, but mere words will never work. It is through our daily actions as they are that we may have some influence. However exemplary our conduct may be at times, if we are ordinarily selfish and hateful in our dealings, we may hardly expect much effect for good. Only if we are good examples through the twenty-four hours of the day, may we expect to bring to our way the people who live and work around us.

We are told that Ananda and Rahula were slower than the other high-ranking disciples to gain enlightenment, but it is inconceivable that they should have been slower than the five hundred who had received their predictions. We can only suppose from all this that we are seeing Shakyamuni's deep consideration. We may feel sure that this view is the right attitude for later followers of the Buddha.

•10• A Teacher of the Law

The title of this chapter does not refer only to monks and priests. Any person who teaches the Law of the Buddha for the sake of others is a teacher of the Law. The chapter is a most important one and has the most intimate connection with our own life in the faith because it indicates the frame of mind of the teacher, particularly the feeling that those of us in these latter days of the period of the Decay of the Law (*mappo*) must have, and points out the merit of right teaching of the Law.

A feature to be noted here first is that beginning with this chapter there is a distinct change of style, for the Buddha's sermons are hereafter directed to the bodhisattvas. The idea that the *shravakas, pratyekabuddhas,* and bodhisattvas were separate orders of being was implanted in all minds, but the Buddha has repeatedly emphasized through nine chapters that such distinctions really do not exist, because all are walking the Way to becoming buddhas. The evidence of this is the prediction of buddhahood for so many *shravakas,* the word *shravaka* being used here in the sense that includes the *pratyekabuddhas.* From this point on, all listeners to the teaching of the Buddha are bodhisattvas.

Any person listening to the teachings may still be the same person, but the feeling in listening changes, and as a result the self-awareness of the person changes. Thus all become bodhisattvas, and for this reason the Buddha shifts his address from the earlier Shariputra or Maha-Kashyapa, who are *bhikshus,* to the Bodhisattva Medicine King, or the Bodhisattva Manjushri, or simply bodhisattvas.

Near the beginning of the chapter Shakyamuni declares that he foresees perfect enlightenment and buddhahood for whoever hears no more than a single verse or phrase of the Lotus Sutra and is moved for so much as a moment to feel in his heart how fine and precious it is.

In our ordinary, everyday world we know from numerous examples how some people accomplish great things because they have had a clear feeling that something was important and worth doing. Without such a feeling and deep concern, many who are interested only in personal gain may accomplish a little something or get to a spot with a little security, but great things are beyond them, and they can do nothing for history to record.

In our religious lives this is all the more true. The teaching of the Buddha is the summit of summits, and whoever hears that teaching and is clearly moved and clearly believes has in himself that which makes unlimited achievement possible. Such is the sense in which the Buddha described the merit of delighting in the words of the sutra even for one fleeting moment.

But to feel this delight in fineness for a moment and then revert to the old self is not the real thing. To be sure, that momentary delight remains at the bottom of the heart, and though unbeknownst to the person it may work its influence, that influence is not so striking. The feeling of that moment must be made to grow, and in being fixed on the mind and heart, its influence becomes great. Veneration and practice are the things that nurture that feeling. Veneration is the offering of heartfelt gratitude for the Buddha, his teachings, and the *sangha,* or community of believers, as expressed in reverence and other actions.

Having stated that any who delight in a verse or phrase of the Lotus Sutra will reach enlightenment, the Buddha continues that those who receive and keep, read, recite, expound, and copy so much as a verse of the sutra will also reach enlightenment. The passage is easy to overlook, so simple does it seem, but it names five important practices that teachers of the Law ought to engage in. First, in receiving and keeping, one must maintain the determination of acceptance always fresh. Through reading, one must study over and over. Through memorization and recitation, one must plant the substance in the heart. Equipped in this way, one is able to explain the teaching for the benefit of others. And finally in the labor of copying, one is actually and symbolically engaged in the effort to spread the teaching throughout the world. Each of these five acts is essential to anyone who would practice the Lotus Sutra.

The great distinction of the Lotus Sutra is its particular emphasis on the positive action of teaching for the benefit of others and of spreading the teaching throughout the world, together with its emphasis on the fact that, without such action, human society can never be saved. This chapter contains the following passage, which is one of the most important:

"If these good sons and daughters, after my extinction, should be able by stealth to preach to one person even one word of the Law-Flower Sutra [the Lotus Sutra], know these people are Tathagata-apostles sent by the Tathagata to perform Tathagata deeds. How much more so those who in great assemblies widely preach to others."

After this there is a remarkable passage in which the supreme quality of the Lotus Sutra is stated and given meaning in a variety of ways. Finally, as the most perfect statement of the Buddha's teachings, it is given a place almost higher than that of the Buddha himself, for though it may be evil to rail at the Buddha, the sin of one who abuses a practitioner of the sutra is greater. The practitioner attains supreme bliss, for the Lotus Sutra is the very foremost of all the sutras, the culmination of the Buddha's teaching. This thought, coupled with the merit of the practitioner, is stated and restated with emphasis, and the perfection of its message is likened in a brief parable to water deep in the earth, which only tireless search and effort may bring to light.

The true believer, then, who would actively engage in spreading the word, must go into the house of the Tathagata, be clothed in his clothes, and be seated in his place. This second major point in this chapter, which shows the right way to present the doctrine, is stated as follows:

"If there be any good son or good daughter who after the extinction of the Tathagata desires to preach this Law-Flower Sutra [the Lotus Sutra] to the four groups, how should he preach it? That good son or good daughter, entering into the abode of the Tathagata, wearing the robe of the Tathagata, and sitting on the throne of the Tathagata, should then widely proclaim this sutra to the four groups."

The four groups referred to here are the four classes of disciples: monks (*bhikshus*), nuns (*bhikshunis*), men and women lay believers (*upasakas* and *upasikas*), respectively. The three terms the abode, the robe, and the throne of the Tathagata give an important instruction, and they are precious, lofty words to be felt with all one's being. They are truly awesome, and their meaning is concisely explained immediately afterward:

"The abode of the Tathagata is the great compassionate heart within all living beings; the robe of the Tathagata is the gentle and forbearing heart; the throne of the Tathagata is the voidness [void] of all laws."

In short we are taught that we are to teach the Law on the threefold footing of compassion, gentle forbearance, and perception of the void. The first two of these need no explanation. The third may require a word, at the risk of some repetition. We may understand the term void here in two senses. First, we may perceive that all existence is void; all apparent forms are but temporary manifestations of this void. This view is of course correct, but to stop at this denial of apparent forms is no way to help mankind.

We must therefore ponder this void from the opposite direction. What we must consider is how all things and forms in the universe, how we ourselves as human beings, are produced from one void that can neither be seen with the eyes nor felt with the hands.

There is a great invisible force, a root life-force of the universe, the working of which produces all things from the void, and all things are produced by virtue of the necessity of their existence. Humanity is no exception.

We ourselves are brought into being in the forms we take by virtue of the necessity to live in this world. If we think in this way, we are bound to feel the worth of being alive as human beings, the wonder of having been brought into this world. At the same time, others are born by virtue of the same necessity to live in this world, and so we are bound to recognize and respect their worth also.

To understand the void in this sense enables us to enjoy the worth and the wonder of living. A true sense wells up in us of the unity of all people as brothers and sisters sharing the same life. So we are taught here that in order to explain the Law to others we must sit in the place of the Tathagata, which is to say that we must ground ourselves thoroughly in understanding of the void.

In summary, then, these three principles teach that whoever would explain the Lotus Sutra must be moved by a spirit of great compassion, be fully grounded in how to perceive the void, and proceed to the task with gentleness and strength of mind, unmoved by concern for what the world may think or do. This is the kernel of this chapter on how to be a teacher of the Law.

• 11 • Beholding the Precious Stupa

The previous chapter closed with the Buddha's explanation of the frame of mind necessary for teaching the Lotus Sutra in the latter days (*mappo*) and the merit of accepting the teaching rightly.

The present chapter opens with an event that immediately follows those closing words. Suddenly a resplendent tower, or stupa, springs from the ground and stands in the sky, and from inside a great voice announces how wonderful it is that Shakyamuni, the World-honored One, is preaching for this great assembly the Law-Flower Sutra—a teaching founded on knowledge of the truth that all living beings alike have the buddha-nature. It teaches everyone the Way of the bodhisattva, and it has the necessary protection of the buddhas. In support of the truth of the teaching, the voice continues that all that Shakyamuni, the World-honored One, says is true.

The listeners are struck with a wonder they do not understand, and the Bodhisattva Great Eloquence asks why it is that this stupa has risen from the earth and why a voice within it has spoken, to which Shakyamuni responds that inside the stupa is the whole body of the tathagata.

We need to note here the great importance of these words. Since tathagata means one who has come of truth, or from the world of truth, the meaning of the whole body of the tathagata's being in the stupa is that the figure of perfect truth is inside.

Truth in this sense is the final and real aspect of the universe. In other words it is the void. In human terms it is the buddha-nature that is man's true face. The stupa, then, is a symbol of the buddha-nature.

It is important to observe that the stupa did not come down from heaven but sprang up from the earth. Heaven is an ideal world removed from mankind, while earth is the actual world in touch with mankind. The buddha-nature is not something given from heaven or the beyond, but rather something dwelling in ourselves, coming from the earth, and so we are shown here that we need only discover this thing for ourselves.

The great teaching of the Lotus Sutra is the Way of the bodhisattva, which, founded upon the truth of the buddha-nature, is to rescue the world through the discovery and development of the buddha-nature present in all people. The buddhas guard this most important of teachings, and because Shakyamuni has for the first time given this teaching for the good of all mankind, he has done the most praiseworthy of praiseworthy deeds: a deed of utmost importance to all generations of mankind. This is the sense in which the great voice from inside the stupa of the buddha-nature speaks.

Now, to return to the text, the Buddha answers the

question of the Bodhisattva Great Eloquence by saying that the voice from the stupa is that of a buddha
called Tathagata Abundant Treasures, from far, far
away in the east, and that when he was still a bodhisattva this buddha had made a vow that upon becoming a buddha he would go wherever the Lotus Sutra
might be preached. He would go there to listen,
appearing in a stupa before the assembled congregation to bear witness to its truth and to give praise.
Moreover, upon attaining buddhahood and leaving
the world, his parting word would be that those who
would worship his whole body should erect a great
stupa.

In this passage, "far, far away in the east" means
that the Tathagata Abundant Treasures is not a
buddha who actually appeared in bodily form in this
world. Truth itself, complete or perfect truth, is here
named Abundant Treasures. Had the Buddha used
such a term as truth itself, or perfect truth, his hearers
at the time, ordinary people, would not have understood his meaning, and so he gave it the human-
seeming form of a tathagata.

The one thing that does not change with time or
place is truth. Since the beginning of the universe,
always and everywhere, truth exists unchanging.
This truth may appear in various forms, but all forms
taken together in one are symbolized in the Tathagata
Abundant Treasures, whose name literally means a
presence of many precious things. His instruction to
erect a great stupa means to make manifest the
buddha-nature of all things. This is the highest form
of veneration of the Tathagata Abundant Treasures,
or truth. For what he desires is that the truth be made
plain as truth. The buddha-nature of all things being

made plain is the expression of perfect truth in this world.

The Bodhisattva Great Eloquence, who earlier had asked who was in the stupa, again pleads with the Buddha, saying that all the congregation want to see with their own eyes the buddha body of the Tathagata Abundant Treasures and urging that by the Buddha's supernatural power they may be permitted to worship it. At this point Shakyamuni explains that the Tathagata Abundant Treasures had made a deep and grave vow. His vow is that when he makes his stupa appear before any of the buddhas who preach the Lotus Sutra, if any of them want his own body shown to the congregation, he will appear bodily when all the buddhas sprung from him are recalled to assemble from the various worlds where they are preaching the Law.

We now need to stop for a moment to examine what this vow meant.

There are countless doctrines of truth in the world, but all of them are only fractional bits of truth. In explaining the real aspect of existence and in explaining that the true nature of mankind is buddha, the Lotus Sutra brings together all truths and shows the complete form of truth, which is no other than the perfect body of the tathagata. Thus a correct explanation of the Lotus Sutra shows this to be a teaching that brings together all truths. Piecemeal explanation of parts is the same as the earlier tactful means of teaching, but this cannot be regarded as the correct explanation of the Lotus Sutra.

Accordingly, attesting to the truth of the Lotus Sutra demanded that all the bits and pieces of the truth scattered throughout the universe be gathered together in one place. This is why the Tathagata Abundant Treasures made his vow that all the buddhas born of his body would have to return and assemble in one place for him to appear.

At this point the Bodhisattva Great Eloquence again speaks for the congregation, asking that they might see these buddhas, and Shakyamuni illuminates the universe in all directions to assemble them. It thus becomes clear that the entire universe, not merely the *saha*-world of Shakyamuni, is filled with emanations of the Buddha's body. The world then undergoes a transformation that at once purifies and beautifies it and makes it spacious enough to accommodate the buddhas now assembling. When all have assembled, Shakyamuni himself rises into the sky and comes to rest in front of the precious stupa.

He then stretches forth his right hand, the symbol of knowledge, and opens the door of the stupa to reveal the Tathagata Abundant Treasures seated motionless, entire, as though in meditation. At once the tathagata speaks, praising Shakyamuni, whose explanation of the Lotus Sutra he has come to hear.

In this, something most important is symbolized. The Tathagata Abundant Treasures, being the totality of truth, sits perfectly still, indicating that truth is everlasting and unchanging. But the truth unmoving, as though in meditation, has no power to change our lives. Only when someone explains that truth so that it moves the hearts and minds of people does it become something that may rescue the human world. This is why the Tathagata Abundant Treasures, being truth, praises Shakyamuni, for it is Shakyamuni who in preaching the truth is setting it in motion. In this way the hope is expressed that the truth itself will be explained, widely understood, and given motion and application.

The Tathagata Abundant Treasures, revealed sitting squarely in the middle of his jeweled throne, slips to one side and offers the other half to Shakyamuni, who then enters the stupa and sits there with him.

In this brief action we may see two things suggested. First, there is destroyed the delusion held by many that Shakyamuni is only the Buddha of the flesh that was born and would die, for here he is shown to be a buddha like the Tathagata Abundant Treasures, and that, while of flesh subject to birth and mortality, he is the everlasting Buddha. This is made plain in chapter 16, but here it is merely suggested. And second, the Law-body, or ultimate substance, represented by the Tathagata Abundant Treasures, and the transformation or mutable body, the human form in which Shakyamuni Buddha appeared, are shown to be of the same order, which is to say that the truth itself and the interpreter of that truth are equally worthy beings.

Now, when all those assembled see the two tathagatas, Abundant Treasures and Shakyamuni, seated aloft on the jewel throne in the stupa floating high in the sky above them, they begin to think the buddhas remotely high and distant and to wish that by transcendent power they might also be gathered up into the sky. And Shakyamuni, at once perceiving their thought, lifts them up in a body, announcing that his remaining time before leaving the world is short and that he must entrust his teaching to the assembly in order that it will continue forever. At this point the material presented in the chapter so far is repeated and ornamented in verse, in the course of which the wonder and merit and great difficulty in the future world of keeping the great lesson of the Lotus Sutra are given attention. For the pleasure it will give the Buddha, the congregation is urged to believe and be resolute in spreading the teaching in the face of all difficulties. Here the chapter closes.

As used in this section the word sky means the ideal. The Tathagata Abundant Treasures is the ideal buddha, but Shakyamuni in his visible body has attained that ideal state and sits alongside the Tathagata Abundant Treasures in the precious stupa. When those gathered here see this, their spirits are moved to strive for that ideal state. This is what we call awakening to the bodhisattva ideal or generating the aspiration to enlightenment. In lifting the multitude to the level of the stupa, Shakyamuni figuratively brings them near this ideal.

The locale of the sermon so far has been Vulture Peak, but here it shifts to the sky, where it remains until the very end of chapter 22, "The Final Commission," after which the sermon is resumed on earth. There is a deep meaning in this shift of scene between two locales for the three segments composing the long sermon of the Lotus Sutra.

The earth is actuality, the sky the ideal. Now any lesson that at the beginning is not taught in relation to actuality is difficult to grapple with and hard to understand. And so the Buddha also began his explanation with actual problems of how to shake off delusion and be delivered from human suffering. Even limiting ourselves to the Lotus Sutra alone, we may see that at the very beginning the Buddha preached the knowledge of how to perceive what our world is made up of, what man is, and what kind of relations are right between one human being and another.

Once this knowledge has become part of a person, he must finally be shown the ideal state, which in the text here is the awakening to the Eternal Buddha that is the great life-force of the universe and the state of becoming one with that life-giving force. In actual life this state is hard to grasp, and awakening is impossible unless the mind is freed of egoism and enters a supernatural world—in other words, a state to be attained by mounting into the sky. Having attained this awakening, it is then possible to return to actuality and to put that awakening into practice in this world. And unless one reaches out to many, many others, unless the rescue of all mankind is achieved, personal salvation is incomplete. This is why the locale of the closing session of the sermon is back on earth. The Lotus Sutra is thus highly rational in structure.

• 12 • Devadatta

In the preceding chapter, "Beholding the Precious Stupa," the great truth was made plain that man's true nature is the buddha-nature. Accordingly, to perceive that one's own true nature is the buddha-nature is the first and highest way to perfect oneself as a true human being. Indeed, whoever fully attains to this perception is none other than a buddha. Therefore any person at all—a wicked man despised by the world or an untaught child—who fully awakens to his own buddha-nature, if only he firmly believes, will become a buddha.

The teaching of awakening to one's own buddha-nature is developed in the present chapter, "Devadatta," which is made up of two parts, the first dealing with a wicked man's attainment of buddhahood and the second with a woman's attainment of buddhahood.

The chapter opens as the Buddha tells of a previous existence, when for long ages he was a king. He had not been content with his life of ease and kept seeking a doctrine of complete truth. For the sake of finding such a doctrine, he determined to give up his entire way of living and announced throughout his kingdom that he would become the body servant of any man who might teach him how all men could be saved.

A hermit came to him and said that he knew the Law-Flower Sutra, by which all people could be saved, and that he would instruct the king if the king would be as good as his word.

The king then and there became the hermit's servant. He gathered fruit and nuts, drew water, attended to all his needs, and even went so far as to lie on the ground in order that his master the hermit might sit and rest on his body. Laboring in this way, he heard the supreme teaching. This story is repeated in verse. Shakyamuni then announces that his own attainment of enlightenment had a distant but major connection with his practice and austerity in this previous existence and that the hermit who had taught him was none other than Devadatta in a previous existence. Owing to this good friendship with Devadatta, he had thus become a buddha and been enabled to save many living beings. He then declares that at a time far in the future and after long practice Devadatta will become a buddha.

Now this Devadatta was a cousin of Shakyamuni and was numbered among the disciples, and though he was sharp of mind, his spirit was warped, and he became opposed to everything, breaking up the harmony of the order and even making attempts on Shakyamuni's life, so wicked a man he was. The listeners are greatly astonished and strangely moved—though the sutra does not say this in so many words—to hear Shakyamuni say that so great a traitor was his own good friend, that it was owing to Devadatta that he had become a buddha, and that at last Devadatta too would become a buddha.

We may wonder here why Shakyamuni described this former existence and said that all was "due to the good friendship of Devadatta." The reason is that to one with so pure a spirit as Shakyamuni all things, whether good or evil, are means to enlightenment. So naturally he felt gratitude for all things in heaven and earth, for whatever transpired about him helped him toward enlightenment. This is a lesson we must learn thoroughly: that all things, both good and bad, are to be seen as means to enlightenment, for which we may be grateful. This is the first lesson of this chapter.

A further question one may ask is why an evil man like Devadatta was also granted buddhahood. Although he was the means of Shakyamuni's deepening enlightenment, this was in no true sense any credit to Devadatta. His evil was not thereby erased. Thus there is no connection between the gratitude to Devadatta and the prediction of his buddhahood.

Shakyamuni abruptly presented this example of

Devadatta as a means of taking his hearers off guard, to impress upon their minds dramatically the truth he had repeatedly spoken: that all people alike have the buddha-nature.

Although the idea that all alike have the buddha-nature may be stated, the actual sense that one partakes of the same nature as the Buddha hardly occurs to the ordinary person. When the close disciples like Shariputra, Maha-Maudgalyayana, Maha-Kashyapa, or Maha-Katyayana are assured of buddhahood, the ordinary person is apt to feel that the likes of such exalted people have nothing to do with him. But as the sermon continues and the five hundred and the training and the trained all get their predictions, the truth begins to come home. Still it is hard to shake the feeling that all those people were advanced practitioners, far beyond oneself.

Then in an abrupt turn the enemy of the Buddha, the evil Devadatta, is given assurance of buddhahood. The hearer, knowing that the Buddha cannot lie, has it brought home to him that if even Devadatta may become a buddha, then one who has never committed such evil deeds must have yet a better chance. Shakyamuni used this brilliant device to bring all men to perceive for themselves their buddha-nature.

Physical and mental desire are the common lot of mankind. The practicing monk must strive completely to separate himself from such desire, but this is quite impossible for people living an ordinary life in the midst of their families. To try to do what cannot be done is against nature, and so ordinary people are taught to turn this desire in favorable directions. This is the Mahayana way. For example, if the desire to make money can be channeled into working for society, the same work and moneymaking may become a force for good.

Devadatta turned his desire as it was into action, and this was evil. But in Mahayana teaching, if desire is diverted toward good, it may work for good. The difference between evil men and good men is merely this. Basically all people alike have the buddha-nature. And so even Devadatta, if through practice he diverted his great desire toward good, might do away with this desire and at last become a buddha. This is the second lesson of this chapter.

We turn now to the last part of the chapter, concerning women.

When the Buddha has finished showing that wicked men may attain buddhahood, the Bodhisattva Wisdom Accumulation, an attendant of the Tathagata Abundant Treasures, thinks that the sermon on self-awareness of the buddha-nature is over and suggests to the Tathagata Abundant Treasures that they return to their own land. But the Buddha detains him and tells him to stay for a while to attend to his disciple Manjushri. At once the Bodhisattva Manjushri appears from the dragon palace at the bottom of the sea—a place we may take to represent the state of a culturally backward people.

The Bodhisattva Wisdom Accumulation greets Manjushri and asks him how many beings he has converted. Manjushri answers that they were countless but that there must be proof. As he speaks, like a cloud rising from the sea, the splendid bodhisattvas he has converted appear, seated upon beautiful lotus flowers.

The Bodhisattva Wisdom Accumulation is struck with admiration and asks what he taught in the sea, to which Manjushri answers, only the Law-Flower Sutra. The Bodhisattva Wisdom Accumulation then presses on and asks if there is anyone now about to attain buddhahood from the teaching, and as Manjushri is answering that indeed there is, the eight-year-old daughter of the dragon king appears and does reverence before Shakyamuni. At this, Shariputra breaks in and informs the girl that the perfect knowledge of the Buddha took incalculable time and is to be attained only after diligent labor and full practice of the Six Perfections, and that a low-brained female with obstacles in her way can hardly accomplish it.

The girl gives no answer except to present to the Buddha a single pearl she holds in her hand—a jewel worth the three-thousand-great-thousandfold world. The Buddha joyfully accepts her gift. The dragon girl then tells Wisdom Accumulation and Shariputra that yet more swiftly than the Buddha's acceptance of her pearl she herself will become a buddha, and at once she appears in masculine form as a buddha presenting the teaching of the Lotus Sutra in a spotless world far away to the south.

Beholding this scene, Wisdom Accumulation, Shariputra, and the entire congregation are greatly moved and receive the truth of this worthy occasion into the depths of their hearts. Here the chapter ends.

Attitudes toward women have been much alike in many countries, but in ancient India there was the hard notion that women were far inferior to men, that they were a body compounded of evils, and that as such they were beyond the pale of redemption. This passage in the Devadatta chapter showing that a woman might in her human form attain to the highest state and be a buddha was an earth-shaking declaration. It is thought that in all of world history this is the earliest clear call for equality of men and women.

Men and women have inborn differences—bodily shape, role in reproduction, distinctive nature, and strengths and weaknesses in the way they work. But men and women thus unlike in form, giving play to their inborn distinctiveness, build congenial households and operate society. Through all this we must not forget that really men and women are equal and alike, and this is the ethical and social ground of male-female equality.

This ground may be understood intellectually, but at the time of the composition of the Lotus Sutra, people still felt deep in their hearts that women were to be looked down on, and this idea was not easily shaken. Shakyamuni, then, went yet one step further to make the identity of the true nature of mankind unmistakably clear by the supreme assurance of the attainment of buddhahood. The idea was thus fully put here that all people, men and women alike, have the same buddha-nature.

One may object that in the text of the sutra the dragon girl does not become a buddha in her female form but is changed into a man to become a buddha. But if we consider the psychology of the Indian people at this period, the point may readily be understood. By the dramatic expression of having the girl change into a man and become a buddha, the congregation, in whom the idea of looking down on women was fixed, was greatly impressed and made to grasp the meaning. But we need not dwell on this.

At first not even Shariputra could believe that this

eight-year-old girl from the dragon palace could then and there become a buddha, and in this we may find an important lesson.

This eight-year-old girl symbolizes the forthright mind and heart of the child, and, as was pointed out earlier, the realm of the dragon palace symbolizes a people at a low level of culture. The pearl worth the three-thousand-great-thousandfold world is none other than faith.

If with the forthright mind and heart of a child we believe in the teaching of the Buddha, then in that instant we melt into and are one with the great life-force of the universe. The universe is ours. Faith indeed is worth the three-thousand-great-thousandfold world.

The Buddha's immediate acceptance of the pearl means that by and through faith one can straightway go through to the mind of the Buddha. The feeling and the response born of this are the direct route to buddhahood.

With the advance of civilization, people tend to manipulate religious teachings solely in the light of reason. Understanding is, of course, important, but reasoning alone has never led to that splendid turning of the mind that comes from sudden perception in the depths of the spirit. The eight-year-old girl from the dragon palace, though not of advanced mind, yet through selflessness of heart and utter faith in the Buddha enters the state of true perception.

It is important for us, too, in setting ourselves to study the teachings of the Buddha, to cast off ready-made ideas, fixed notions, and gripping emotions and to be as receptive as a sheet of clean white paper. This is the lesson we must draw from the account of feminine attainment of buddhahood, which continues from this chapter into the next.

• 13 • Exhortation to Hold Firm

There is a brief passage at the opening of the chapter where numbers of bodhisattvas declare their devotion and determination to keep the teaching alive down through the ages. Then Shakyamuni's foster mother, Mahaprajapati, and his erstwhile wife, Yashodhara, are both in turn assured of buddhahood. Here, then, following on the preceding chapter, the doctrine of women's attainment of buddhahood is fully stated. We may find two lessons in this situation. These two women were *bhikshunis,* or nuns, of high attainment and accumulated virtue; they had the direct instruction of the Buddha; and yet they were not given assurance of buddhahood until the last—even after the culturally backward little dragon girl, who was an indirect disciple, having been taught by Manjushri.

The first lesson we may find here is identical with the lesson of Ananda and Rahula, namely, that it is difficult to influence people who are very close—in this case the woman who had reared Shakyamuni from infancy and the woman who had been his wife and borne him a son.

Whereas with the dragon girl and Manjushri the simple student-teacher relationship meant direct acceptance of the Law, the physical involvement of people as close to Shakyamuni as his foster mother and wife meant a less smooth acceptance. This is often the case.

We may thus see the deliberate delay in prediction here as a means of teaching this truth. There is no sense at all that the two nuns were inferior to the dragon girl.

The second lesson here is that so long as the teaching is rightly transmitted, it does not matter who imparts it. Nor, so long as the teaching is straightway accepted, does it matter how uneducated the person is who receives it, for all gain the same perception of the Buddha. We who are living today may be most grateful for this teaching. For salvation is at hand for whoever straightway accepts the Law with a clean mind, and it does not matter that we are not taught directly by Shakyamuni himself. Now, over two thousand years later, any person of any nation or any race may freely have all that is here.

The title of this chapter, "Exhortation to Hold Firm," applies to the vow that the assembled bodhisattvas made with great force: to protect, practice, and preach the illustrious teaching, even at the risk of their lives. They had been profoundly moved by the sermon of the Lotus Sutra, in particular the truth made clear in Devadatta that all mankind alike had the buddha-nature.

While the title means an urging of acceptance and retention of the teaching, it becomes clear from the actual content of the chapter that "urging" is not the meaning, for the language throughout is rather that of avowal of personal determination. Inasmuch as firm personal determination and personal practice are essential to leading others, and to urging others on, this title has deep significance.

The closing eighty-line verse section of the chapter is of particular importance. The Chinese original of this is in twenty lines, each consisting of four phrases, from which circumstance the passage is frequently referred to in Japanese as the "twenty lines of the chapter on holding firm." Many people are familiar with the great Japanese priest Nichiren's self-awakening and assertion that he was born into this world with the heaven-ordained mission of preaching the Lotus Sutra in the latter days of the Law (*mappo*) and that every particular of his own experience was described in this passage.

The meaning of the passage is that reverence for the Buddha and reverence for this sutra, in which the highest of his teachings are presented, are one and the same, and therefore any persecution or hardship attending protection and dissemination of the sutra is to be borne with courage. There is to be no concern for body or life, only concern lest there be a single person left untouched by the highest teaching. There shall be effort to preach this Law everywhere, without fear of contempt that comes from misunderstanding or of persecution arising from the enmity of those of other beliefs or of the power of false saints enjoying the protection of the mighty, who would consciously disregard the truth and strive to stamp it out. The apostles of the World-honored One thus vow rightly to preach the Law with all their strength, and the Buddha may therefore abide in peace.

Three potent enemies of the Lotus Sutra are cited here, and although in our time of freedom of religious belief they are not the source of the kind of persecution believers in the Lotus Sutra underwent in India two thousand years ago, or that Nichiren experienced in Japan seven hundred years ago, still today such enemies exist.

First are the herd, the arrogant of the world, who, neither knowing nor having read the Lotus Sutra, yet regard its teaching as fanatical and disparage its believers. In the past, half the fault on this account has lain with believers in the Lotus Sutra, and so we must reflect and exercise restraint lest we assume an attitude of self-righteousness, use the teaching for political ends, or preach only its material benefits in this life. Always we must model ourselves on the true and essential meaning and with inner force clothed in gentleness maintain the true believer's attitude as we preach and explain the teaching.

Second are the religious, the arrogant of religion, people of other religions and sects who are simply hostile and make no effort to see the truth of the Lotus Sutra. Tolerance is one of the most important qualities of religion, particularly Buddhism. It is for religion to forgive the errors people have made and to embrace all people. The so-called religious people who are immediately hostile to other religions and sects because of superficial differences in doctrine or different practices of belief are not religious at all. If we ourselves as practitioners of the Lotus Sutra are critical of such people and fight them, then we ourselves are trampling under foot the spirit of tolerance. Rather we must be forbearing to the last as we exert ourselves to the utmost extent in order that such people may awaken to the true meaning of religion.

Third are the pretenders, the arrogant of pretense, those people in high places in religion or the scholarly world who enjoy popular regard and who, intoxicated with their condition and to protect their own position, defame the true teaching. A really great person who sees the truth will boldly support it, but one of narrow mind is all too apt to turn flatly away from a newly found truth and to besmirch lofty teachings. The fact that such people are seen as high and mighty makes it easy for them to make use of the credit and regard they enjoy, and the very greatness of their influence means that the possessors of the third form of arrogance, the arrogance of pretense, are the most vicious.

We need not resist these forms of arrogance directly. It is enough to proclaim and spread the truth we believe as we tread the right Way. Truth will always triumph. Meanwhile, if any of us should reach high position, we need to be on guard against falling into such arrogance and always with freshness of mind, suppleness of heart, and youthful vigor maintain a receptive attitude.

The watchword of practitioners of the Lotus Sutra, "Give no thought to body or life," is derived from the superb couplet in this passage:

> We will not love body and life,
> But only care for the supreme Way.

To the contemporary person, to give no thought to body or life does not of course mean to have no care for this life itself. It means, rather, not to dwell on personal benefit—to have no regrets for time and labor in the good cause and to have no fear of what others may think or say about what one does.

If one asks why a person should feel and do so, the answer is that he gives thought to the truth. So long as there is a single person as yet untouched by this highest teaching, he must care. Such a state of purity of feeling is the making of the true practitioner of the Lotus Sutra.

•14• A Happy Life

Whereas in the preceding chapter the bodhisattvas have declared their determination to stand firm in the face of all obstacles and harm, the present chapter deals with the Buddha's advice to be always at ease in preaching the Law. For this purpose he offers specific instructions on the state of mind to be achieved. He gives assurance that belief in the teaching of the Lotus Sutra and practice of this teaching will enable everyone to attain a peace of mind by which all difficulties may be overcome. By the law of nonduality of body and mind, this peace of mind pervades the body and is manifest in the way of life.

The Buddha addresses his instructions for the bodhisattvas to Manjushri, and in a long and detailed sermon explains the fundamental precepts that should govern the behavior of a bodhisattva. A bodhisattva, the Buddha says, must abide in a state of patient endurance, be gentle in mind, be not overbearing, follow right reason, and conduct himself with composure. All things are to be seen as ultimately void, and conduct is not to be governed by concern with appearances. All appearances are to be seen as arising because they must arise in accordance with the law of cause and effect, and nothing is to be judged and arranged by means of differentiation or discrimination.

Specific, detailed admonitions or precepts follow, and I pick up ten out of those that are of special importance today. Summarized and simplified, these are as follows: The bodhisattva (1) does not in any sense of self-seeking approach or associate with persons of position or influence; (2) is alert not to be taken in by extreme ideas; (3) is careful in relations between men and women, and, when explaining the Law to the opposite sex, is particular neither to become sexually aroused nor to provoke desire; (4) whenever acting alone, is ever mindful of the Buddha, remembering always to maintain the sense of being with the Buddha; (5) when explaining the Law or reading what is written of the teachings, takes no pleasure in digging out the defects of others or in detecting fine points of error in the texts; (6) has no contempt for others who explain the teaching (an obvious admonition for people of the same persuasion, but equally applicable to those of other faiths); (7) is circumspect in criticizing either the good or the bad in others when the matter is teaching the Buddha's Law; (8) never replies at random to any question, however difficult, responding always in the true sense founded upon Mahayana teachings; (9) is attentive to the capacity of the hearer to comprehend the true sense of the Great Vehicle, drawing upon actual instances, parables, and other means of making the meaning clear; (10) is moved by the vow to free all living beings from their suffering, being mindful of compassion for them, feeling the buddhas as benevolent fathers, and seeing the host of bodhisattvas as great teachers.

The parable of the gem in the topknot, the sixth of the seven parables in the Lotus Sutra, appears in this chapter, and, like the others, it teaches an important lesson. A certain powerful king chastised minor kings about him who refused to obey him. He rewarded his valorous captains and soldiers with lands, or even cities, or ornaments and jewels from his person, reserving to himself only one precious jewel dressed into the hair of his topknot. Because this one jewel was all too precious, he could not give it away lest his followers be astonished and confused.

The Buddha's supreme teaching in the Lotus Sutra had been deferred until now for a similar reason. Much had already been taught, and by this teaching many had gained such rewards as attaining stability of mind, delivery from human suffering, and relief from all desire. Only the truth of the Lotus Sutra remained to be presented. But to have presented this truth prematurely would only have confused.

Then, just as at last the king gave away the jewel in his topknot to his victorious soldiers, so the Buddha, when all had reached a sufficiently high level of perfection, gave the ultimate reward, the highest teaching embodied in the Lotus Sutra.

A superficial reading of this parable allows us to see only praise of the Lotus Sutra as the highest teaching, together with the fact that presenting the world with such teaching is a rare occurrence, but beyond this there are other lessons.

First, we may note that the king had numerous other valuable things, but all these were but possessions pertaining to his body, while the bright gem alone of all his jewels pertained to his head. Now the head is the abode of the animating spirit or mind that directs the body. All people use their bodies, but harnessing the spirit is most important, though this is difficult because the spirit is intangible. Moreover, merely to harness the spirit without elevating it does not make for an admirable human being. The lesson we should draw from this parable is that mankind's highest aim pertains to the head and means elevation of the spirit to attain buddhahood as the ultimate aim.

Second, the parable tells us that as the ultimate teaching the Lotus Sutra is like the spirit in human life, to give it to people not yet prepared to understand it can only give rise to confusion and puzzlement. We may readily see in ordinary life that this is exactly the case with study in any discipline or technique. To attempt to teach the highest level of anything to a rank beginner can only puzzle, for the beginner is not equipped to listen or follow and can only drop away. And so, though from the point of view of the teacher what is taught first may be ridiculously simple, the lesson must begin with easy things. Then, as the student learns and progresses to later stages, the teacher may approach and at last deal with the ultimate matter. This course is clearly suggested by the parable.

In another way, as an admonition to the learner or practitioner, we may see that basic practice is essential if one is to attain to the ultimate. People today, particularly young people who have received higher education, are unwilling to go into such basic practice and want to go at once to an advanced stage. This sort of thing can only lead to trouble, just as disaster so often overtakes the inexperienced mountain climber.

Whether in life or in work, it does not do to do things halfway. Basic practice is essential to achievement. This again is something we must learn from the parable of the precious jewel.

• 15 • Springing Up out of the Earth

With this chapter we begin the closing half of the sutra—that is, the part dealing with the Law of Origin, (chapters 15 through 28), in which the ultimate substance of the Buddha (and the ultimate substance of mankind, which is the same) is made clear. This Law of Origin is the underpinning of the Law of Appearance (chapters 1 through 14), or the derived teachings set forth in the first fourteen chapters.

The first portion of this chapter forms an introduction to the Law of Origin, while the latter part, combined with all of chapter 16 and the first half of chapter 17 (the one chapter and two halves) gives us the essence of the Law of Origin.

As the present chapter opens, the World-honored One has completed the part of his sermon in chapter 14, "A Happy Life," and hordes of bodhisattvas from other worlds step forward and offer to spread the teaching in this *saha*-world after the Buddha's extinction. But the Buddha assures them that there is no need for their help, for from of old there are countless bodhisattvas already in this world whose duty it is to preach the Lotus Sutra. No sooner has he uttered these words than the surface of the earth breaks apart and countless bodhisattvas, in figure all resembling the very Buddha, rise up from the crevices.

This host of bodhisattvas is led by four outstanding ones—by name, Eminent Conduct, Boundless Conduct, Pure Conduct, and Steadfast Conduct—who come forward to salute the Buddha and are in turn addressed in a free and familiar fashion.

Those who had earlier assembled to hear the Buddha are puzzled by this development, and their questioning is expressed in a long address by the Bodhisattva Maitreya, who asks where these splendid creatures have come from and what kind of persons they are. The Buddha answers simply that they are those whom he has taught in this *saha*-world and led to enlightenment and that they have until now dwelt in a space beneath the *saha*-world. But the fact of the matter, it develops, is that from a time far, far in the past he has been engaged in instructing all this host of bodhisattvas.

This seemingly simple answer only puzzles the Bodhisattva Maitreya and all the other questioners, for they cannot understand how in the forty-odd years since Shakyamuni's enlightenment it has been possible to bring such numbers of beings to a state of perfection so near that of the Buddha himself. Yet no one close to the Buddha over these years has ever seen one of them. The chapter closes with a poetic repetition of the perplexity in which all now stand, as the Bodhisattva Maitreya presses Shakyamuni to explain and sweep away their doubts.

If the Bodhisattva Maitreya himself was confused in this way, there is little wonder that we in this latter age of *mappo* should be puzzled. In point of fact, however, the Buddha, responding as he did, was employing a device. By stating an apparent contradiction and raising questions in the minds of his listeners, and then in one stroke explaining the difficulty, he was able to leave a lasting impression. The explanation comes in the following chapter, "Revelation of the [Eternal] Life of the Tathagata," and by way of making this easier to understand, some explanation is needed here.

The expressions "taught in this world" and "instructed from a long time past" suggest two different ways of viewing a person. The first means viewing that person as a physical being with his own personality— that is, from the viewpoint of seeing the phenomena. The second means viewing that person as a being identical with oneself in having the buddha-nature, or the great life-force of the universe—that is, from the viewpoint of wisdom that penetrates the real aspect of things. The former is the way of viewing distinctive forms and their differences. The latter is the way of viewing identical being and equality. The right way to view mankind includes both aspects.

If you view a bodhisattva from the former viewpoint, he can be called a bodhisattva by influence: one who is influenced by Shakyamuni's teaching and is engaged in practice. But if you view the same bodhisattva from the latter viewpoint, he can be called a bodhisattva of the essence: one who, since the remote past, has been taught by the Eternal Buddha and is part of him.

Bodhisattvas by influence and bodhisattvas of the essence are in ultimate substance one and in no sense different, though it is possible to see here a vast difference between the splendor of the bodhisattva of the essence and the lowliness of the bodhisattva by influence. This, however, is merely a way of expressing the difference between those who have a self-awareness of being bodhisattvas of the essence and those who do not.

Accordingly, in our own time those of us who learn the teachings of the Buddha, practice them, and work for the salvation of people are bodhisattvas by influence. But if there were one who from the bottom of his heart had the awareness that he was one with the Eternal Buddha, though his actions might be like those of the bodhisattva by influence, such a person would be a bodhisattva of the essence. In outward appearance the forms of faith of the two, the bodhisattva by influence and the bodhisattva of the essence, are alike, but if one enters into the inner substance of that faith, a difference of level is to be found that becomes apparent in the work of instruction and salvation.

There are different ways of viewing the sudden emergence from out of the earth of the throng of bodhisattvas described in this chapter, but we may observe three points of particular note.

The first is in Shakyamuni's declining the offer made by the bodhisattvas from other worlds and entrusting the teaching to those who sprang up out of the *saha*-world. The lesson here is simply that only through the work and effort of people living wherever they may be is it possible to achieve peace and build a happy life.

The second is in the way in which the bodhisattvas, enjoying the state of enlightenment and dwelling in a space under the *saha*-world, broke through the ground at the sound of the Buddha's voice. Now those bodhisattvas dwelling in the space beneath this *saha*-

world, though most certainly people of this world, were living in the pleasure of awareness of the void but had not as yet been moved to exercise that awareness for the salvation of the human world. Awareness of the void in human terms means seeing that the true nature of mankind is identical with the buddha-nature. So they were certainly aware of this truth, but they only took pleasure in this in themselves and did not turn outward to work for others. Such as these may indeed be fine people without blemish, but they do not serve for the salvation of living beings.

There is, then, an absolute necessity for such as these once and for all to break through the ground. In other words they must experience life in actual society; they must plunge into the grime and dirt in which humanity is struggling and feel directly humanity's suffering and torment. Only in this way may they really come to lead people and to save them. It does not do merely to deal in ideas, for without being in touch with reality one cannot deliver mankind.

The third is in the conduct element that formed part of the name of each of the four outstanding bodhisattvas who led the throng that sprang up out of the earth—that is, Eminent Conduct, Boundless Conduct, Pure Conduct, and Steadfast Conduct.

The first half of the Lotus Sutra was given over largely to the teaching of reason and truth, the teaching of wisdom. But upon completion of that half of the sutra, we had the abrupt appearance of a countless throng of bodhisattvas who were doers. Any teaching without application in practice, in conduct, is nothing. It must move on to the stage of action. The true bodhisattva is the doer who applies his knowledge of the true aspect of all reality, the statement of which truth

is the theme of the first half of the Lotus Sutra. He is
the doer who, in his compassionate conduct, exem-
plifies the truth of the buddha-nature identity: the
kind of person who makes the teaching of the Buddha
meaningful in this world. Since this so precisely
applies to us who are alive today, it is important to
take the message to heart.

•16• Revelation of the [Eternal] Life of the Tathagata

The doctrine of the real aspect of all
existence was explained in chapter 2, "Tactfulness,"
the pillar of the first half of the sutra. What the
doctrine amounts to in brief is that root and branch
are after all alike. In other words this is to say that
although apparent forms we see with our eyes display
differences in accordance with a fixed law, root and
branch, from first to last, are alike void. This is a cold
scientific or philosophical truth. But simple understanding of this truth alone does not lead then and
there to human happiness.

Accordingly Shakyamuni developed this truth step
by step in human terms, namely, that the ultimate
substance of mankind is the buddha-nature. Even
though at the very beginning he had clearly stated this,
it was hard for the congregation at large to grasp the

truth, and so he made use of parables and tales of past existences to draw his listeners on, by suggestion preparing their minds to accept the truth.

Now in this chapter on the eternal life of the Buddha, the truth is clearly revealed. Here it is stated beyond doubt that the ultimate substance of the Buddha is the everlasting life-force of the universe, none other than the Eternal Buddha. It is further stated that mankind and all other things are but part of the Buddha—children of the Buddha, so to speak. In this way the cold perception of the void becomes charged with human warmth as people are stirred to gratitude upon realizing, deep inside, that they live wrapped in the compassion of the Eternal Buddha. At this stage comes true happiness and a sense of the worth of being alive.

The philosophical perception taught in the first half of the Lotus Sutra is now, in the second half, given a spiritual lift and takes on the ineffable quality of a religious teaching. This chapter thus becomes the heart and soul not only of the Lotus Sutra but also of all the sutras.

The truth is explained rationally, but in the parable of the physician's sons it is put in terms easily understood by all. The parable forms such an important part of the chapter that it is well to consider the essentials of this part of the sermon in terms of the parable itself.

The parable tells of a doctor renowned for his knowledge and skill with medicines, for he can cure any disease. This doctor has many children, and once when he has to go away to attend to some matter, in his absence the children drink some of his poisonous medicines. Such an event would never have happened if he had been at home, but children will be children, and this is the result. As the poison begins to work, they throw themselves on the ground in agony. At this point the doctor comes home. Some of the children are not so badly affected, but some are completely out of their minds. Still, they are all overjoyed to see their father again. They welcome him home, tell him how foolish they have been, and beg him to cure them and save their lives.

The doctor at once sees their state and sets about compounding curative herbs of pleasing color, taste, and smell. He gives his children the medicine he has compounded, promising them that it will take away their pains and cure them. The children who are not so badly affected and have not lost their senses take the medicine and are immediately cured, but the ones in whom the poison has worked deeply will not take the very medicine they have begged for. Being out of their minds, they do not like the color and smell and will not take it.

The physician sees that he must take extreme measures if his poor children are to be saved, for the poison has completely overcome their senses.

He then gathers the children together and tells them that he is getting on in years and must soon die. Still, he has affairs to attend to and must go away again. He will leave the medicine he has prepared for them and urges them to take it. With this he sets out and has not been gone long before he sends a servant back with word that he has died.

The children are shocked and thrown into sorrow at this news. For the first time they keenly feel their desolation, and the shock restores their senses. The medicine their father has left now seems pleasant to look at and smell. They swallow it down and are promptly cured. At this point the father they have all thought to be dead comes home, alive and well.

The doctor in this parable is the Buddha, the children ourselves. The poison is various desires, and the good medicine is the teaching of the Buddha.

Ordinary people are subject to all kinds of desire, and the prime reason for this is that they think that only what they can see with their eyes really exists and that what they can't see doesn't. Indeed the minds of all of us are taxed and in pain on account of our seeing our own bodies, money, and other material things, as well as all the events occurring around us, as things that really exist.

Shakyamuni taught that all visible or apparent forms in the world are but temporary appearances brought into being by combinations of causes and conditions. If these causes and conditions did not exist, neither would those visible forms, and different causes and conditions would produce other visible forms accordingly. On the basis of this truth he enunciated the doctrines summed up as the Twelve Causes, the Four Noble Truths, the Eightfold Path, and the Six Perfections. Through these teachings many were enabled to set aside delusion and attain to a peaceful state of mind.

Now so long as the superb leader Shakyamuni was near at hand constantly to teach and instruct, all was well with those he led. But it is a melancholy fact that when a leader is gone, bit by bit many an ordinary follower will revert to what he was before. The average person, who thought that only what he could see really existed, was all too likely to stray from the path once Shakyamuni Buddha, who could be seen, had entered nirvana, or died as a physical body, even though the Buddha as life-force of the universe was and is always at hand.

Shakyamuni was concerned about this, and through the parable of the poisoned children he made abundantly clear the doctrine that the Buddha exists forever and is imperishable. Thus it is that though the leader may pass on, if only the truth he taught remains, men may be saved by it.

Just as the children in the parable, in their father's absence, did as they pleased and brought pain on themselves by inadvertently taking poison, so other living beings, in the absence of the Buddha in person, have brought suffering on themselves by living as they pleased. In the parable the father returned from the dead, so to speak, when he came home, and even the children who, like people swayed by various desires, had lost their senses from poison were overjoyed to see him again. They were like anyone, for however far one may stray from the path, in man's heart of hearts the buddha-nature remains intact.

The Buddha, like the physician-father, compounded a variety of precious medicines: a medicine to put aside delusion, a medicine for gaining true wisdom, a medicine to awaken a spirit of dedication to others. These were his devices of teaching. There were some who accepted them at once and were thereby saved, but there were numerous others who paid no attention and would not touch the medicines left for them. Being out of their senses, they found no virtue in them, mistaking their fragrance for stench and their color and taste for something foul. They would not touch them, for they were infatuated with the pleasures of various desires. To them the teachings of the Buddha were cramping, and they had no wish to listen to them.

This is shallow mankind's selfish way. The Buddha,

then, resorted to an extraordinary device to open people's eyes. He hid himself for a time where he could not be seen.

Historically Shakyamuni entered nirvana, which is to say that as a physical body he died. At this people felt suddenly left alone, and in their hearts there arose a fierce sense of devotion to a great leader lost. As powerful as a thirsty man's want for water, an urge to seek after the Buddha welled up in their hearts. In the verse passages of the sutra this thought is expressed as longing and thirsting.

People recover their senses as soon as such an intense feeling fills their hearts. They awaken. At this they realize that they must do something, and then with a will they leap to the teaching left for them and willingly take their medicine.

This longing and thirsting is not just for the visible Buddha. It has a more general or abstract sense. It often happens that a person who has never been interested in gods or buddhas, always intent on the affairs of daily life, suddenly faces some crisis. He finds then that he wants something to lean on or that he has enough of material things. He feels that something is missing and wonders if there isn't something that can give satisfaction to the spirit. Now what such a person is looking for, whether he knows it or not, is some god or buddha, for something to lean on, for something that can give satisfaction to the spirit.

And so either the historical Buddha or the Buddha whose being is abstract will serve. The important thing, if one's spirit is to be cleansed, if one is to be delivered, is to long for what can truly bring deliverance, to long for it with all the intensity of a man perishing from thirst. In this one point religion differs from the teachings of philosophy or ethics. The fine teachings of philosophy and ethics are easy enough to grasp with the mind, the surface of the mind. And if everyone understood them in this way and acted accordingly, there would be no problem. But in fact things don't go that way. Though much may be known on the surface of the mind, there are things hidden in the recesses of the mind that are not so easily dealt with, and unwittingly people are led astray by these things and in consequence act badly. This is why the hidden mind also must be cleansed, for without such cleansing there can be no deliverance. Religion and faith accomplish this for us.

In the parable the children were awakened when they were overtaken by longing and thirsting for their father, and when they had recovered their senses, their father came back home. In general terms what this means is that any being may, if he is only alert, know that the Buddha is ever there.

The ultimate substance of the Buddha is the eternal, imperishable life-force, and never for an instant is this not at our sides. No, not at our sides, for it is a mistake to think of it as beside us; rather, the Buddha abounds within and about us all. We ourselves are of one substance with the Buddha.

Thus it is that if the Buddha seems not to be present, it is merely because we have forgotten or lost sight of the presence. Man has little abiding interest in infinite existences. How many people are always conscious of air or the sun or water? Only when something happens, particularly when there is want, do we remember how precious these things are.

We commit the same error with the Buddha. The ultimate substance of the Buddha is the basic life-force that calls into being, animates, and moves all things. And so since to live by the law of this life-force is to be free in the mind and ever happy, why should anyone ever forget, act contrarily, and bring suffering upon himself?

If we have a deep awareness that we are animated by the Buddha, the life-force of the universe, if we are alive to the truth that as long as we are animated by the life-force of the universe the right way to live is by its laws, and if only we live according to the teachings of the Buddha, which are founded on these laws, then we may live always with the greatest confidence. Whatever pangs of life there may be, it will be as though they actually did not exist.

This is the true way to live as a human being, and this is the great lesson of this chapter.

• 17 • Discrimination of Merits

The previous chapter set forth the principle that the ultimate substance of the Buddha is the basic life-force that calls all things into being, animates, and moves them and that it is an everlasting presence abounding within and about us all. The present chapter takes up the merit of clear perception of this principle, breaking it into twelve parts or stages, and states in detail the way to live in right faith.

Without going into these twelve stages one by one here, let it be enough to say that the meaning is this: if we hold the faith that we are animated by an eternal life-force without beginning or end, the power of deepening that faith and of extending it to others wells up without limit. Then if that faith is thorough-going enough, we are granted the supreme merit of knowing that we will at last attain the identical ultimate awakening experienced by the Buddha.

Clearly no ordinary practice is going to lead to such an attainment of buddhahood. As told in this chapter, there were bodhisattvas who practiced through eight lifetimes before attaining that state. But simply to know that by right faith and true endeavor we will at some time reach the same state as Shakyamuni is a vast source of light to ourselves and to all humanity. If only there is this light, then every human life takes on meaning and is joyous.

When a life is passed in a succession of empty pleasures and sorrows—making money and losing it, loving and being disappointed in love, reaching a position only to lose it through some small failing—there well may be a sense that every moment is full, but in retrospect at the moment of death such a life, which has been swayed by a narrow egoism that chased after shadows, will seem utterly empty.

How totally different, though, is a life in which there is a firm backbone of faith—even a life that superficially seems no different from such a vain life of recurring pains, sorrows, and joys! For with this backbone, with the certainty that, whatever the ups and downs, every step on the way is that much nearer the state of the Buddha, the most painful life may be lived pleasantly and ended happily.

Our lives do not stop with this life. The life of the Buddha is imperishable, and our own lives that are part of that life are likewise imperishable. To realize—even merely to think—that this life, the next, and the next, on and on eternally, must be a repetition of everyday joys and sorrows is enough to make most say, "No more." But with true faith, with the awareness that every step brings us that much closer to the state of the Buddha, then, however long the journey, it is always full of interest, of hope, of fulfillment. This indeed is the great merit won by the true believer.

Yet the effort of the true believer does not end with himself alone, for while his effort is toward the state of the Buddha, he strives also to bring all those he can into the way he treads. For as the number of true believers swells, mankind as a whole is raised up, and the world is brought closer to becoming itself that highest paradise, the Land of Eternal Tranquillity and Light. In summary, this is the meaning of the twelve stages of merit enumerated in this chapter.

The concluding division of the Lotus Sutra runs from the last half of chapter 17 through chapter 28, the end of the sutra. The main themes of this division are the merits of right faith, the state of mind necessary to right faith, and Shakyamuni's command to his disciples, including our latter-day selves, to preach the right faith to later generations.

The present chapter, "Discrimination of Merits," explains the merits of faith. They are merits of the spirit, as are those of the first half of the next chapter, "The Merits of Joyful Acceptance." But beginning with the last half of that chapter, merits affecting our persons and our daily lives are taken up.

Some may say that there is no need to attend to these merits, that if one studies and fully comprehends what is taught in the crucial sixteenth chapter and the two half chapters on either side of it, it is enough to have complete faith that, like the life of the Buddha, man's life is everlasting and imperishable.

And certainly anyone who can do just this is com-
mendable. But in fact such complete faith is hard to
attain, and there is a question as to whether one in
ten thousand, or even one in a hundred thousand, can
attain it. The sad fact is that the average person takes
the ideal state described as a world far, far removed
from the likes of him or her. And so after all, if the
teaching is truly to be felt, it must be put in terms of
things close at hand to everyday life. This is of great
importance in the concluding division of the Lotus
Sutra.

Again the average person tends quickly to slack off.
Most people readily see how fine a thing the teaching
is and understand this with their heads, but they get
lazy. However, if they have right faith, practice it in
their persons, and actually advance upward as taught
in the scripture, and if they constantly read and recite
that scripture, then their faith will constantly be re-
newed and never give way to the tendency to slacken.
This is of equal importance in the concluding division.

Again, Shakyamuni specifically directed even people like ourselves to announce his teaching to others.
This is a thing to be grateful for. And every time we
look upon his words and see into his thought, we are
lifted up and lent new courage and steadfastness.
This is of final importance in the concluding division.

And so for the 99,999 in 100,000 that are average
people, the concluding division is indispensable, and
with all due humility we must read it with the same
intensity as those parts that form the essence of the
teaching proper.

The T'ien-t'ai patriarch Chih-i, of China, reduced
to easily understood and memorable form the essential matter of this chapter as it bears on the mental
preparation of the believer. He described this prep-

aration in nine short phrases under two headings:
four faiths and five categories. The items of the four
faiths are sometimes referred to as the four faiths of
the presence—that is, four stages or levels of faith that
describe the proper conduct of the believer during
Shakyamuni's lifetime. The stages of the four faiths of
course apply equally today.

The first stage of the four faiths is momentary faith
and understanding. It is important to believe in and
understand, even for a single moment, the limitless-
ness of the life of the Buddha, for this is to understand
the real aspect of all things. It is the great leap of the
spirit.

Second is overall appreciation of the meaning of
the teachings. A step beyond the first, this means to go
beyond momentary faith in and understanding of the
immeasurable life of the Buddha to a broad appreciation of the great meaning contained in the teaching.
It means that just as the life of the Buddha is eternal
and imperishable, so also are our own lives in that
they are one with the Buddha's. Only because we are
lost in clouds of illusion do we not see this. If one by
one we dispel these clouds, then without fail we perceive that we are entirely one with the Buddha.

Third is broad study and ministry, by which is
meant what the believer should be and do. Beyond an
overall understanding and appreciation of the truth of
the teaching, the believer learns the broad teaching of
the Lotus Sutra, plants it firmly in mind, gives devotion and thanksgiving to it, and goes on to tell it to
others and bring them to the Way of the Buddha.

Fourth is deep faith and clear perception, by which
is meant that with deepening faith in and understanding of the immeasurable life of the Buddha, the believer gains the certainty of the Buddha's constant

presence. With this comes a view of life and the world perfectly in accord with the teaching of the Buddha and a capacity to live in a state of joy in that teaching.

In turn, the five categories are sometimes referred to as the five categories after extinction because they describe the proper conduct of the believer after the Buddha's extinction and the five merits that are related to this conduct.

The first of the five categories is the first attendant joy. By this is meant the stirring of a sense of joy upon learning of the existence of so precious a teaching as that of the immeasurable life of the Buddha and understanding what this means. This is faith, and the thought is dealt with at some length in the following chapter, "The Merits of Joyful Acceptance."

Next comes reading and recitation. While the first attendant joy in itself is proof of true faith, the teaching must be firmly implanted in the mind by intense study and recitation.

The third category is preaching. The urge to tell others about it is a natural outcome of close knowledge of the priceless teaching of the Buddha. In telling others, the believer betters his own condition, and his merit is the greater because of influencing others for good.

Fourth comes auxiliary practice of the six degrees, the six degrees being another way of speaking of the Six Perfections of a bodhisattva: donation, keeping the percepts, perseverance, assiduity, meditation, and wisdom. What is meant by auxiliary practice is that at the same time that a person accepts, reads and recites, and preaches the Law (that is, the teachings) he also practices the Six Perfections. In so doing, the bodhisattva moves on to a yet higher state.

Finally comes full practice of the six degrees, and

with the attainment of this category of complete practice, the practitioner is near the full knowledge and enlightenment of the Buddha.

Chih-i's statement of the four faiths and the five categories, part of which is reviewed here, is in words that compress the exact expression to be found in the sutra. The reader may therefore find it hard at first to identify the elements of the four faiths and the five categories described. But they are there, and because Chih-i's terse expression gives us a set of easy-to-use terms, it is important to match them with the passages from which they are derived and to remember them.

•18• The Merits of Joyful Acceptance

The theme of this chapter is stress upon the merit of first attendant joy, with a detailed explanation of it. The reason for this repetition is that the joy attendant upon the teaching, with heartfelt gratitude for it and delight in it, is the primary and indispensable element of faith.

The chapter opens with a question from Maitreya about the happiness attendant upon hearing this sutra after Shakyamuni's extinction. The Buddha replies at length, saying, in paraphrase, "Let us suppose that someone has been to a meeting for an explanation of the Law, and that, moved by a spirit of gratitude and happiness, he tells someone else as well as he can what he has heard. And let us suppose that the one he has told is equally moved by an attendant joy and that he tells someone else. Then let us suppose that this process is repeated until the teaching reaches the fiftieth person, who likewise is moved to gratitude. The merit of this fiftieth one is hundreds of millions of times greater than the enormous merit accumulated by a very, very rich man who has spent his entire life in giving alms. Now if the merit of the fiftieth hearer is of this order, how much greater is the immeasurably infinite merit of those who heard the message at the first assembly."

As we read this today, we can understand the great merit of the first hearers easily enough, for they are in an atmosphere of faith and are hearing the message from the mouth of a persuasive leader versed in the Law. But when, in the absence of skillful speech or any atmosphere of faith, the word has passed from one layman to another and another on to the fiftieth, then what is left of the message is only the bare bones. But even the bare bones of the Lotus Sutra are such that they cannot fail to impress, even at fiftieth remove.

There are two reasons that the merit of the impression conveyed by the message even at such remove is greater than the merit of a rich man who has spent his life in almsgiving. One is that the spiritual joy that springs from hearing the True Law is a treasure beyond compare. The other is that the joy developed as the message passes from one person to another becomes an infinite force.

Returning once more to the text, we find the thought developed—quite apart from the attendant joy—of the enormous merit of even momentary presence at a sermon to hear the teaching of the Lotus Sutra, and of the still greater merit of urging others who come later to sit and hear or share a seat.

The meaning of this is the importance of the tie, or manner of encounter, with the Law. While it is true that we all have the buddha-nature, without some tie or encounter to awaken us to it, it is of no avail. And so initial contact with the teaching is a prime and necessary condition. It is for this reason that encounter is so worthy a thing and that bringing others to such an encounter is still more worthy.

This chapter, then, teaches something of prime importance to the believer: readiness first to respond with joy upon hearing the teaching, coupled then with a resulting desire to share that joy immediately with others, to preach the message of the Lotus Sutra, the smallest part of which is filled with meaning.

•19• The Merits of the Preacher

Continuing the thread of thought of the preceding chapter, this chapter proceeds at once to deal with the merits of the eye, ear, nose, tongue, body, and mind that any good man or woman will attain from any one of five practices of teachers of the Law: receiving and keeping, reading, reciting, interpreting or explaining, and copying the sutra. With the beginning of the verse passage repeating the virtues that accrue to the eye of the earnest believer, it becomes clear that these five acts are acts of the preacher of the Lotus Sutra, and hence the title of the chapter. As each of the six senses or faculties is treated, the manner of expression becomes so highly symbolic that the reader today may well get a very odd feeling. So it is essential to get to the underlying truth that is expressed.

In Buddhist doctrine it is a matter of course that a change of heart results in a visible change in life. It is out of the question for the heart to change and life not to. It is certain to. The change in life that comes of a change of heart by faith is termed merit.

Now merit is evident not only in the mind and heart but also in physical and material life. Since man's mind, body, and material surroundings are all alike derived from a uniform void, it is by no means odd but perfectly reasonable for the body and its material surroundings to change in consequence of change in the mind and heart. It is therefore neither reasonable nor scientific to affirm merit or merits of the mind and deny physical or material merits.

We have seen great advances in medicine on this score. The latest psychic and somatic, or psychosomatic, medicine has found and demonstrated psychic activity to be a cause of many ills as varied as eye trouble, skin trouble, heart trouble, stomach trouble, high blood pressure, hives, morning sickness, abnormal menstruation, and other troubles that seem at first to have nothing to do with the mind. Accordingly, when the way of thinking is altered, the illness corrects itself, a clear indication that mind and body are not divisible. They are closely bound together and are not separate things. There is nothing odd about this.

Again, there is nothing odd about a person who has

through faith undergone a change of heart, a change in his or her way of thinking, having the blessings of money or other material things come his or her way. With a change in the bearing of the mind, an entire change in attitude toward work and life necessarily follows, and improvement and change for the better are natural consequences.

Moreover, the entire atmosphere surrounding the individual filled with true Mahayana belief—awareness of being part of the Eternal Buddha—is different. For such an individual is bright, filled with confidence, and has a sense of positive dedication. In consequence the people around such an individual see him or her in a different light. They are touched by a charm they cannot explain. They feel trust. Thus it is that work goes well and material blessings naturally follow.

More than this, as stated here and in the preceding chapter, the body and countenance also change. This is no more than is to be expected, for mind and body are one. Now while it is true that a noble, happy countenance and person are the expression of that person's virtue, they are more usually the outcome of previous generations over a long period of time. Lincoln's well-known remark had it that a man had to take responsibility for his own face after the age of forty, but the fact is that a man has still greater responsibility for the faces of his descendants.

The merits described here are an expression of the results or consequences of Mahayana faith, and so when such consequences become manifest, one should take them as they come. There is no need whatever to hold the perverse notion that since faith is wholly a matter of the spirit, nonspiritual merits tarnish a spiritual life.

What is tarnishing is faith that has as its object

benefit in this life. More than tarnishing, it is wicked and conducive to retrogression. Faith should have as its object reconstruction of the mind and spirit, and if this is achieved, it is well then to accept without fuss any physical and material merits that may follow.

Toward the end of the chapter there is one sentence not to be overlooked:

"If he refers to popular classics, maxims for ruling the world, means of livelihood, and so forth, all will coincide with the True Law."

"He" means the preacher of the text, and the statement means simply that such a person will spontaneously conform to the True Law when he teaches about daily life, when he discusses government, or when he gives directions in business.

The True Law has very much to do with society at large and is by no means limited to individual spiritual concerns. And so it lends true life to secular law. If this were not so, it would ultimately have no power to deliver all of mankind. We must mark this point well.

•20• The Bodhisattva Never Despise

The great root of human unhappiness is the mistaken idea or illusion that the physical body is the self. As long as this illusion exists, care for this physical body comes before everything, and one's first thought is always for its satisfaction. People other than this self are always secondary, and so it happens that, with so many acting the same way, people take from each other and push each other around. The result is endless unease, anxiety, and pain.

If mankind is to be rescued and if society is to be truly at peace, the illusion must be destroyed and replaced by awakening to the truth of the buddha-nature in all men. Certainly it is desirable to try to make people better by regulating their everyday attitude and conduct, getting them, through teaching, to leave off bad things and do what is right, but this method alone will never be effective. Only when there is awakening to the truth of the buddha-nature will the urge to do wrong disappear, for the awakened individual is incapable of doing what is ugly or shameful.

Such awakening does not stop with the individual, moreover, but goes beyond in that there is awakening also to the basic truth that all are one with the great life-force of the universe. Thus, out of a welling up of a sense of brotherhood and sisterhood, people are able to get along together.

This chapter illustrates this principle in relating the history of a bodhisattva of the ancient past whose name was Never Despise. Never Despise, by the single repeated act of revering the buddha-nature in others, achieved the enlightenment of a buddha and brought numerous others to that same enlightenment. This Bodhisattva Never Despise, whenever he saw someone else, was in the habit of saying, "I do not despise you, for you will become a buddha." He was, in a word, seeing straight through to the buddha-nature. But people did not understand him, were angered by his stupidity, and threw rocks at him and beat him with sticks. Never Despise, though, only retreated and from a distance called back to his persecutors that they would be buddhas.

From steadfast practice of this one act, the Bodhisattva Never Despise was able, as death was near, to perceive the universal and human truth set forth in the Lotus Sutra: to gain awareness of his own infinite life. Through countless rebirths he preached this truth, and at last he became a buddha.

It is made plain here that this bodhisattva was none other than Shakyamuni himself in a previous life. In other words, Shakyamuni himself became the Buddha by virtue of awareness of the buddha-nature of all human beings and by persevering cultivation of this awareness.

This cultivation began simply as reverence for the buddha-nature in others, but when these others finally began to be aware of their buddha-nature, the bodhisattva began to preach this truth as doctrine. We ourselves must watch and learn from this. Setting out from recognition of and reverence for the buddha-nature in all people, we must move on to preaching the doctrine of the truth and cultivate the buddha-nature in society at large. From just such active effort as this may the individual's understanding be deepened and the world made a better place.

Like the Bodhisattva Never Despise, we must continue this effort long and earnestly with unchanging faith. It will never do, because there are no immediate results, to give up after a little effort and to throw in the sponge in despair at the state of the world. Neither oneself nor the world will be saved this way.

Human nature is everlasting and imperishable, and

so with firm determination we must continue the great work through countless births and deaths. This is yet another lesson taught by the example of the Bodhisattva Never Despise.

• 21 • The Divine Power of the Tathagata

Here the mysterious powers of Shakyamuni Buddha and multitudes of other buddhas are displayed, and the point is powerfully made and impressed upon the assembled hearers that though until now the preaching in the Lotus Sutra has been various, there is just one single truth.

The short chapter opens as the assembled bodhisattvas do reverence and assure the World-honored One that after his extinction they will preach the Lotus Sutra widely and perform the acts of devotion due it. At this point Shakyamuni puts forth his broad, long tongue until it reaches the Brahma heaven, and every pore of his body radiates light that reaches every corner of the universe. This is the first of a sequence of acts that follow in rapid succession and are described in swift strokes. Each of these has meaning, and here I point out those meanings, much slowing down the rapid pace at which they are described in the sutra.

The outstretched tongue symbolizes that everything preached by the Buddha is true, infinite, and one.

As we have seen, at first Shakyamuni had appeared in the *saha*-world and, as a buddha inhabiting that world, taught a derived or apparent truth to guide human conduct. People had looked up to him as the Buddha and worshiped him with heartfelt devotion. But then he taught the full original truth that he was the Eternal Buddha, which is to say, the great life-force of the universe, and that true deliverance rested in firm awareness that this Original Buddha without beginning or end was the life-giving energy.

These being the facts, some may wonder which of the two Buddhas should be the object of devotion and veneration. The act of stretching out his tongue was a demonstration afresh that the apparent Buddha and the Original Buddha were not and are not separate. Shakyamuni, a manifestation of the life-giving energy that is the Eternal and Original Buddha, appeared in this world for the salvation of living creatures, and so in origin there is no distinction between the historical and apparent Shakyamuni Buddha and the Eternal Original Buddha.

Had Shakyamuni not appeared in this world and preached the Law, we would never have known of the existence of the Original Buddha. Therefore there is no way of determining which of the two, the apparent or the original, is prior and to be worshiped above the other. This is why, through the figure of the human Shakyamuni, we must think on and make the Eternal Buddha the object of our devotion and worship. The demonstration of divine power in the outstretched tongue signifies that the two truths are one faith.

The radiation from Shakyamuni's entire body of

wondrous, many-colored, beautiful light that shone into every corner of the universe symbolizes that the light of truth, though it may seem various in that it is of different hues, is yet light that dispels every shadow of perplexity.

The heart of the doctrine taught in the first half of the sutra as derived truth is the Ten Suchnesses, which appear in the highly philosophical statement made near the beginning of chapter 2, "Tactfulness." The statement says that only a buddha together with a buddha can fathom the reality of all existence and that all existence has such a form, such a nature, such an embodiment, such a potency, such a function, such a primary cause, such a secondary cause, such an effect, such a recompense, and such a complete fundamental whole. All these, it is to be implied, derive from one uniform void. When we arrive at the section where the original truth is stated, however, the existence of the source that brings all things into being is described not with the icy word void but with name of a warm, all but flesh, life-giving energy, the Eternal Original Buddha.

Though these may seem in a way to be two different truths, in fact they are the same fundamental truth, expressed first in a philosophical sense, then in a religious sense.

The singleness of the two truths is symbolized by the felicitous sign of radiation of light from every pore of the Buddha's body, multihued, but reaching every part of the universe and dispelling darkness.

Shakyamuni Buddha and all the other buddhas then cough in a body. To cough in this case means to set forth the teaching, and for all to cough at the same time means no more or less than that all the teaching returns to one. Accordingly, the simultaneous coughing means that in terms of the preaching throughout Shakyamuni's lifetime the three vehicles (that is, *shravaka, pratyekabuddha,* and bodhisattva) are as such the One Buddha-vehicle, or, in terms of the Lotus Sutra only, the two truths are one teaching.

Shakyamuni and all the other buddhas then snap their fingers, again in a body as one. This action, in Indian custom, meant understanding, agreement or commitment, and mutual assurance, and what the buddhas all commit themselves to and assure each other of is that together they will spread the teaching far and wide.

Their commitment stems from a sense of boundless compassion for living beings, or, in terms more easily understood today, a full sense of being one with others. If we think closely on the teaching of the Lotus Sutra from its very beginning right on through, its object is to awaken and make firm a sense of being one with others. The philosophy of apparent truth, that the real aspect of existence is the void, in effect also teaches that any self is one with all others. The teaching of the original truth that all people are brought into being by the Original Buddha that is without beginning or end similarly teaches in the deepest sense oneness with others.

If all people attained this realization and made it part of their lives that individual human beings do not subsist separately but are fundamentally one substance, then indeed affection would overspread human relations, and we would have a truly peaceful world.

The ultimate aim of the Lotus Sutra was to teach that self and others are one substance, and when all the buddhas together snapped their fingers, it meant that they committed themselves to spread through the *saha*-world the spirit that the two truths are one man, by which is meant that all men are one identical substance.

Hard upon the action of the buddhas' coughing and snapping their fingers, heaven and earth respond by shaking six ways. The meaning of this is that as all were profoundly moved, they could not but manifest their feeling in action.

This action is the practice of the bodhisattva. In the first half of the sutra, which teaches apparent truth, the Buddha urges practice of the Six Perfections of a bodhisattva. In the second half, in which the original truth is shown, as the truth comes home of the oneness of self and others, the believer can only move on to the bodhisattva practice and urge to save others. Thus the six-way shaking of the earth signifies that there is one bodhisattva practice whereby the two teachings are made manifest in the world.

Next, by the divine power of the Buddha, the entire throng of all living beings in the universe is given the infinite vision not only of Shakyamuni Buddha and all the other buddhas but also of innumerable bodhisattvas. If we translate this occurrence into the language of today, we may see it as symbolizing that though individual capacity to accept the teachings now shows remarkable differences from person to person, the time will come when surely all alike will attain the same enlightenment. This is the great vow and assurance we have from the Buddha. Thus the infinite vision of the divine gathering seen by all living beings in the universe signifies the Buddha's prediction of future uniform capacity for all. The Buddha's mysterious power will assuredly bring this to pass.

As all living creatures are given this infinite vision and look upon the figures of the buddhas and bodhisattvas, their ears are filled with the sound of heavenly voices urging them to look up in gratitude and pay homage to Shakyamuni Buddha for preaching this highest teaching of "the Lotus Flower of the Wonderful Law, the Law by which the bodhisattvas are instructed and which the buddhas watch over and keep."

This chorus of voices of the gods in the sky, reverberating in the ears of all creatures, is a moving revelation from heaven, a revelation that this very teaching of the Lotus Sutra is the supreme truth, the giver of life in the universe, the maker of harmony, the bringer of true repose.

If we translate the sense of this awakening into contemporary language, we may understand it to mean simply that all the various religions in the world today only clutter the way to mankind's common well-being but that in the future, without fail, all religions and learning will converge in the teaching of the Buddha.

Final truth, as best, can only be one, and so if all human beings move upward on the Way, though only bit by bit, they must arrive at last at the one teaching. This has been the interpretation of the meaning of this passage since early times.

At this point, to return to the text, upon the command of the voices from the heavens, all the living beings of the universe turn toward the *saha*-world, the palms of their hands together in reverence, and raise their voices to chant, "*Namah* Shakyamuni Buddha!"

Buddhism is in origin the teachings of the human Shakyamuni Buddha, and so it is impossible to speak of Buddhism apart from the person of Shakyamuni. The reader will recall that in chapter 16, dealing with the life of the tathagata, Shakyamuni made clear that he in his apparent body alone was not to be thought of as the Buddha, for the Buddha had existed from before, and the true body or substance of the Buddha was the great life-force of the universe. If we put these two things together, then there is nothing surprising about all the creatures of the universe hailing Shakyamuni Buddha and worshiping him.

As true human knowledge advances, it is bound to recognize the truth of Shakyamuni's teaching, and men cannot but take refuge in it. In the language of the sutra, all beings dedicate themselves to the Buddha, for this is the meaning of "*Namah* Shakyamuni Buddha." When the world reaches this stage, there will no longer be wicked men or stupid ones, for every man and woman after his or her nature will be exemplary and live correctly by virtue of the teaching of the Buddha. In such a future state mankind will be one, and the foretelling of this is in the passage where all beings of the universe lift their voices as one to sing, "*Namah* Shakyamuni Buddha."

At this, precious things rain down from every quarter upon the earth and come together to form a lovely canopy over the place where the buddhas are. This occurrence signifies an act of veneration in the form of offerings to Shakyamuni Buddha from all the creatures of the universe. Offerings of veneration take different forms—material, laudatory, and practical— and the highest is that in which every act accords with the spirit of the Buddha. No other act of veneration expresses higher appreciation of the Buddha or gives the Buddha greater joy. This is what the lovely canopy formed by all those precious things means.

In our world today human action is good, bad, and indifferent, but a day will come when every act conforms to the spirit of the Buddha, and here we have the prediction of this future state when action will be one with the Buddha.

Then in a final tableau the worlds of every quarter are united in one buddha-land. Here it is foreseen that out of the one truth all mankind will build a world of great harmony, that there will be one truth, that one buddha-land will prevail.

All these mysterious appearances in this chapter symbolize the truths and predictions I have enumerated here. It is important for us to pay close attention to the idea of oneness that pervades all. This is the spirit of the One Buddha-vehicle, and in this sense the chapter is climactic.

The chapter ends with a repetition in poetry capped by a hymn of praise for the Lotus Sutra, which, though the historical Buddha Shakyamuni may be extinct, yet bears the true message to all the world.

• 22 • The Final Commission

The final commission spoken of here means an entrustment and a call for help. Shakyamuni strokes the heads of all the bodhisattvas and entrusts them with the great work of transmitting the treasured enlightenment to people coming later, calling upon them to preach the Law single-mindedly and cause living beings far and wide to benefit.

In response the bodhisattvas are filled with the

highest joy and three times declare their determination as they happily undertake the difficult task ahead. We must note this well, for it is the prime point of this brief chapter. We latter-day bodhisattvas must take to heart this joy in favor bestowed and happiness in the face of a difficult task ahead.

With this chapter we come to the end of a major section of the Lotus Sutra. This is the close of that portion of the sutra, beginning with chapter 15, in which the perfect truth of the Buddha's ultimate substance or true body and its working is stated. After this we return from such ideal truth to the apparent actuality. In other words, the setting of the Lotus Sutra shifts from the assembly in the sky to Vulture Peak. We should note here that Shakyamuni is said to have preached the Lotus Sutra first at the assembly on Vulture Peak, then at the assembly in the sky, and last once again at the assembly on Vulture Peak.

• 23 • The Story of the Bodhisattva Medicine King

The teaching so far has made clear the truth. Now we come to the matter of real practice. It is a special difficulty for the ordinary person to know how to get everyday action to square with a lofty truth. There is no better way to do this than to observe and follow the example of the bodhisattvas, who are but one step removed from being perfect buddhas and who stand for particularly fine forms of virtue or exemplary action.

Living beings are best encouraged to right action by models close to them, and this and the next few chapters are essentially presentations of just such models or examples.

The first figure to appear is the Bodhisattva Medicine King, who had vowed to heal the sicknesses of mankind. This bodhisattva's dedication and self-sacrifice in a former life are described in order to show him as a virtuous model of veneration of the Buddha and his Law. In his former life the Medicine King had been a bodhisattva named Loveliness—one that all creatures rejoiced to look upon—and in serving the then Tathagata Sun Moon Brilliance, he had heard the truth of the Law-Flower Sutra and in twelve thousand years of ardent practice had reached a high state. By mysterious powers he had caused the heavens to rain flowers and incense as an offering of veneration, an expression of devotion and gratitude for Sun Moon Brilliance's teaching the Law-Flower Sutra. He wished, however, to make yet a greater offering with his body, and so after drinking fragrant oils and anointing his body, he set fire to himself and burned. He burned for twelve hundred years, and the light of his burning illuminated the world.

When this offering was complete, the bodhisattva gained life and was born a prince to the king in the land of the Tathagata Sun Moon Brilliance. As soon as he was born he worshiped the tathagata, who then announced that that night he would enter nirvana and that he counted on the prince to spread the Buddha's Law throughout the world. The tathagata then entered nirvana.

The prince—the Bodhisattva Loveliness—wept,

cremated the tathagata's body, collected the ashes into eighty-four thousand vessels, and placed them in as many stupas throughout the state. Still dissatisfied with his offering, he burned his arms, which already were aglow with stunning virtue. The light of this fire kindled worthy spirits in many, but after seventy-two thousand years people lamented to see that their great leader and instructor was deformed in that he had lost both arms. The bodhisattva announced that though he had given up his arms, he was confident of everlasting life, and at this his arms were made whole again.

We may gather three important lessons from this tale. The first is that there is no higher human virtue than the spirit of self-sacrifice. The second is that there is no higher form of offering than practice. And the third is that far from ruining the self, self-sacrifice really makes the self count for something.

• 24 • The Bodhisattva Wonder Sound

With the conclusion of the passage on the Bodhisattva Medicine King, Shakyamuni emits streams of light—the light of knowledge—from the top of his head and from the circle of white hair between his eyebrows. This light penetrates distances far to the east to a land named Adorned with Pure Radiance, where there is a buddha called King Wisdom of the Pure Flower Constellation Tathagata. A disciple, the Bodhisattva Wonder Sound, addresses this buddha, announcing that he wishes to go to the *saha*-world to worship Shakyamuni Buddha and talk with the great bodhisattvas there.

The Tathagata King Wisdom assents but warns that the *saha*-world is a foul place; that the body of the Buddha is short and small; that all the bodhisattvas are of small stature; that, compared with King Wisdom and Wonder Sound, the Buddha and bodhisattvas are so little that it would be tempting to take them lightly; and that this would be a mistake. By way of illustration he points out that his own enormous height and Wonder Sound's, together with Wonder Sound's body of resplendent gold, are going to make the earthly Buddha and bodhisattvas look small and insignificant indeed.

Whereupon, after various preliminaries, Wonder Sound arrives at Vulture Peak, prostrates himself before Shakyamuni and greets him. He then asks if the World-honored One will allow him to see the Tathagata Abundant Treasures. Immediately after Shakyamuni has relayed this request, Abundant Treasures appears and praises Wonder Sound for coming to pay homage to Shakyamuni.

At this the Bodhisattva Flower Virtue questions Shakyamuni about this odd occurrence. Shakyamuni responds that in a past time Wonder Sound had paid homage to a buddha named King of Cloud Thundering and that from the merit of making music for twelve thousand years and making an offering of eighty-four thousand vessels of treasure, he had acquired the unusual powers Flower Virtue is wondering at. Moreover, Wonder Sound's present body is by no means his only one, for he has appeared in many forms in countless places everywhere to preach the teaching to multitudes of people.

All are profoundly impressed, and Wonder Sound, having accomplished his mission, then returns with his retinue to his own land.

Such is the rough outline of what is described in this chapter. The land Adorned with Pure Radiance stands for an ideal world. The ideal, of course, is a creation of the mind, a place of shining light with a buddha and bodhisattvas of gigantic proportions and surpassing beauty. The actual world, the *saha*-world, is hardly comparable, being a foul place, and even the Buddha and his bodhisattvas seem but pitiful things.

But mindful of the advice of the King Wisdom of the Pure Flower Constellation Tathagata, Wonder Sound paid heartfelt homage to the Buddha of the *saha*-world. The meaning of this act is that Shakyamuni's effort to build an ideal world on earth was far worthier than the mere ideal itself. So long as the ideal is only something plotted out in the mind, it is only a dream. Its worth comes only in realization, in endeavor to bring the ideal to reality. This is the first major lesson of this chapter.

Wonder Sound's playing music and his offering of eighty-four thousand vessels of treasure also have meaning. Making music is a symbol of causing word of the truth to sound in people's hearts, while the offering of so vast a quantity of treasure means the transmission of the Buddha's countless teachings to the people of the world. Transmission of the truth taught by the Buddha is certainly the greatest offering we can make to the Buddha. Shakyamuni was demonstrating this here, and it is the second major lesson of this chapter.

If we understand this, then perhaps the meaning of

Wonder Sound's being in many bodies and preaching the Law everywhere will also be clear. Right in our own midst there are countless Wonder Sound bodhisattvas; in fact, we ourselves, if we but preach the Law with true words, are none other than manifestations of the Bodhisattva Wonder Sound. With this awareness, how great an impetus and inspiration are we given to spread word of the True Law! This, then, is the third great lesson of this chapter.

• 25 • The All-Sidedness of the Bodhisattva Regarder of the Cries of the World

The main subject of this chapter is Shakyamuni's explanation to the Bodhisattva Infinite Thought of why the Bodhisattva Regarder of the Cries of the World had such a name.

It is easy in reading the chapter to think of the Bodhisattva Regarder of the Cries of the World as an object upon whose power, quite outside and apart from the individual, it is possible to rely for salvation. It is of highest importance, however, to see that this is not so but that in fact he is a symbol of knowledge of the truth. Now, exactly speaking, this knowledge of the truth means realization of the middle truth that visible forms are neither the void nor the temporary but a commingling of the two. Applied to the human condition, this means free and liberating knowledge that makes it possible for the person who has it to fit exactly into any situation, while at the same time preserving his or her identity and distinction.

The Bodhisattva Regarder of the Cries of the World was possessor of such knowledge of the truth. He was also possessor of vast compassion that made him ready to accept the sufferings of others in their stead.

Knowing the truth, thinking on the truth, and acting in accord with the truth—this course and no other is the true way to be saved. Further, to save others, we must, out of a spirit of compassion, be self-sacrificing, for thus we may lead them into the path of truth. This is what really is taught in this chapter in the detailed account of deliverance from seven perils by holding in mind the Bodhisattva Regarder of the Cries of the World.

People in olden times had difficulty in grasping so abstract an idea, and this is why the Bodhisattva Regarder of the Cries of the World is presented in the Lotus Sutra as a beautiful, gentle being endowed with surpassing powers of perception, such that he observes the sounds of the world, knows every move, sees what everyone desires, and so, in compassion, appears in what are described as thirty-three guises to rescue people from their every pain. Holding such a being in mind brought salvation as the mind responded to the truth.

We today ought to think on the superb character of the Bodhisattva Regarder of the Cries of the World and try to make ourselves like him. To emulate the bodhisattva passionately will see us through whatever troubles come and will lead us to lend a helping hand whenever we see others in trouble. This is really the main lesson of this chapter.

A further point not to be overlooked is the way in which the Bodhisattva Infinite Thought is so moved by the great virtue and power of the Bodhisattva Regarder of the Cries of the World that he offers up his necklace. Regarder of the Cries, in accepting it, at once divides it, giving half to Shakyamuni the World-honored One and half to the stupa of the Buddha Abundant Treasures. What this means is that the great virtue and power of the Bodhisattva Regarder of the Cries is due equally to the truth of the buddha-nature, which the stupa represents, and to Shakyamuni, the one who explains that truth. We may here see quite plainly that it is a great mistake to think we will be saved merely by praying to the Bodhisattva Regarder of the Cries of the World.

• 26 • Dharanis

All who heard, including the not even human representatives of the spirit world, were moved by the blessing of the Lotus Sutra and now vowed in the strongest terms to protect the teachings of the Lotus Sutra and its followers, and to this end many pronounced spells. This chapter tells how certain of these spells, which are called *dharanis*, were offered to safeguard the sutra and its followers. These "all-preserving true words" were secret words with power in themselves to frustrate evil and further good, and since their power resided in their form, they were not translated when the sutra was translated into Chinese but remained in transliterated Sanskrit, in which form they are found in the English translation.

The *dharanis* in this chapter are made up almost entirely of the names of deities or epithets for them, and as words addressed to the deities, they sought through the power of the words to win response from the beings of the spirit world. This is all somewhat removed from the basic meaning of Buddhist teachings, but the mysterious workings of *dharanis* are something I have experienced so often that I cannot but feel there is some deep spiritual significance in them.

• 27 • The Story of King Resplendent

Here we have the history of King Resplendent, his queen consort, and the princes his two sons. The consort and princes are adherents of the Buddha's Law and desire to get the king to give up his preoccupation with other teachings and recognize the rare excellence of the Buddha's Law. The buddha of the time is one Thunder Voice Constellation King of Wisdom. The princes have heard his preaching of that loftiest of things, the Law-Flower

Sutra, and they ardently wish to get the king also to listen. They consult their mother, who advises them that nothing short of a miracle will work.

Accordingly, the princes go before the king, leap into the air, and walk about in the sky. They shoot fire and water out of their heads and feet, sink freely into the earth, and do all sorts of incredible things. The king is astonished, and when he asks them where they have learned such godlike powers, they inform him that their master is the Buddha Thunder Voice Constellation King of Wisdom, who teaches the Law-Flower Sutra. The king forthwith wishes to see this buddha, and the overjoyed princes, not wanting to lose the opportunity, go to their mother and get her permission to leave home and devote themselves to study of the Way under the buddha.

Thus it is that the influence of the princes brings the king, the consort, ministers, court ladies, and many people of the country to the buddha to hear the Law. The buddha assures King Resplendent that he will gain enlightenment as a buddha, and the king, upon hearing this, makes over the kingdom to his brother and with all his retinue leaves palace and home for the faith.

After long practice the king attains high state in the teaching and reports to the buddha that it is owing entirely to his sons the princes that he has come to this. The buddha confirms that indeed this is true and that a good friend and instructor is certainly the worthy cause that brings many to the buddha and moves them to seek the buddha's knowledge.

We should not take the miracles performed by the princes literally, for what is meant here is that, through faith in the Buddha's Law they had studied, their character had altered, and in consequence their conduct in daily life had undergone a complete change. This was apparent to their father, and the demonstration in actual conduct was what proved the merit of the Buddha's Law and roused their father's interest.

While it is important, in leading people, to preach the Law of the Buddha, what really works is demonstration in action. This is particularly so when the people we try to reach are in our own families or where we work, for whatever we may say about the Law, unless our conduct wins admiration, far from winning people over, we are likely to make others despise or doubt the merit of that Law. This is why the story takes the form it does, and the princes' mother is a wise woman in commending demonstration. Still, their father the king is admirable too in that he is ready to set aside his prejudices and turn his ear to the truth. One who would grasp the truth must have just this kind of mental flexibility.

There is yet another important lesson here in the way the king's faith affects his ministers, household, and subjects. The right faith of a person in a position of leadership has vast influence, certainly, but there is also a serious problem in such influence.

Faith must begin with a matter of individual choice, and faith is tarnished whenever politics or authority is involved. But when a respected leader has faith in the True Law, many people are affected as a matter of course, and there is nothing tarnished or tarnishing about the working of such an influence. In fact, it is a most wholesome influence of exactly the right kind.

Right faith, then, is something to be desired in people who are in positions over many others. They need exert no pressure, for the quality that the True Law calls forth in their persons will inevitably affect those under them for the better.

• 28 • Encouragement of the Bodhisattva Universal Virtue

Here we are told how the Bodhisattva Universal Virtue came from far in the east from the realm of the Buddha Jeweled Majestic Superior King in order to hear the Lotus Sutra. He was so moved by what he heard that he graphically described to the buddha how in future generations he would guard and protect those who received and kept the teachings. In turn, the buddha praised him and announced that he, the buddha, would likewise guard and protect any who did as the Bodhisattva Universal Virtue did. The chapter is thus an overall encouragement to give heart to practitioners of the Lotus Sutra far in the future, in the latter, declining days of the Law.

There is deep meaning in the appearance in this closing chapter of the sutra of the Bodhisattva Universal Virtue. Universal Virtue is the bodhisattva of the virtues of truth, concentration, and practice, and his appearance, mounted upon the white elephant king, symbolizes the preeminence of thoroughgoing practice.

In the early part of the Lotus Sutra the principal bodhisattva was Manjushri, the bodhisattva of knowledge. Midway, notably in chapter 16 on the life of the Tathagata, Maitreya, the bodhisattva of compassion, appeared. The appearance here at the end of Universal Virtue, the bodhisattva whose major attribute is practice, is thus significant. The meaning of this is clear: the hearer of the Lotus Sutra gains knowledge of the real aspect of existence from the part of the sutra that deals with derived truth. He is then awakened to the truth that all living beings are animated by the compassion of the Eternal and Original Buddha. This is the theme of the part of the sutra that deals with original truth. Finally, here, he learns that the teaching not put into practice is nothing. If we understand this, then we have already grasped the meaning of this chapter.

There is, however, one extremely important statement in the chapter that is not to be overlooked. After greeting the Buddha, the Bodhisattva Universal Virtue asks how good men and women are to gain the truth of the Lotus Sutra after the Buddha's extinction. Shakyamuni answers that there are four requisites to its acquisition: "first, to be under the guardianship of the buddhas; second, to plant the roots of virtue; third, to enter correct congregation; fourth, to aspire after the salvation of all the living." We may understand here that we must have faith that we are ever watched over and minded by the buddhas; that in our daily lives we must do good deeds and foster virtue and goodness in ourselves; that we must associate with others in right service to the teaching; and that we must be animated by a desire to deliver all people in the understanding that true salvation means salvation with everyone else.

Here, concisely stated in a form anyone may understand, we have the essentials of the teaching that were explained in detail earlier. Even people who may have been put off by the profundity of the teachings of the Lotus Sutra may here very well get the feeling that they too can make it. This is a most appropriate conclusion to the Sutra of the Lotus Flower of the Wonderful Law.

PART THREE

The Sutra of Meditation on the Bodhisattva Universal Virtue

As indicated by its title, this work, which takes its departure from the closing chapter of the Lotus Sutra, makes the Bodhisattva Universal Virtue its central figure. But because of its special emphasis on confession, it is sometimes referred to as the Sutra of Repentance.

By meditation on the Bodhisattva Universal Virtue is meant the practical way to perceive the excellence of the bodhisattva, to attune the mind to his spirit, to fix the mind on the Way of the Buddha, and to attain to the form of practice of this bodhisattva.

The sutra repeatedly explains how the body of the Bodhisattva Universal Virtue is actually to be seen, by which is meant nothing more or less than attunement of the mind to the spirit of the bodhisattva. Inability to reach this state calls for reflection upon conduct and confession of failings.

Then, even though the believer may indeed see the body of the bodhisattva, practice and effort must not stop, for only by going on to see the body of the Buddha may practice become perfect.

Thus full confession is explained as thinking on the true aspect of reality. The true aspect of reality, the real aspect of existence, is the ultimate void. Single-minded thought and full understanding of this truth bring the believer to a state of oneness with the mind of the Buddha, and all sins, like frost or dew in the sun, are dispersed by the light of wisdom.

To think in such philosophical terms, however, is hard for ordinary people, and so at the end of the chapter we are instructed in a more down-to-earth way of thinking. After an enumeration of the confessions appropriate to the citizen or lay believer, the final instruction is this: "to believe deeply the causes and results of things, to have faith in the way of one reality, and to know that the Buddha is never extinct. . . ."

These words are a most fitting summing-up of Buddhist teaching.

The law of cause and effect, which is meant by "the causes and results of things," is not only the scientific principle that pervades the physical universe but also the truth that forms the core of the basic Buddhist teachings.

Then, whether we are conscious of it or not, it is the truth that every human being walks the one road toward becoming a buddha, and this is the way of one reality. There may seem to be many, many surface differences in the teachings of the Buddha, but the one reality, the one truth, binds all on the Way to buddhahood.

And finally to know that the Buddha is never extinct is to know that the Eternal Original Buddha is the great, imperishable life-force of the universe and that we are brought into being by this life-force and are part of it.

If this threefold faith stands unshakably in our

minds and hearts, then every one of us can attain complete freedom and salvation. There could hardly be a more fitting conclusion to the Threefold Lotus Sutra than these golden words.

Glossary

arhat   Literally, "one who is worthy of respect or veneration." (1) One who is free from all illusions and has achieved personal enlightenment. (2) The highest stage of a *shravaka*.

Avici hell   The hell of "no interval" (*avici*), or uninterrupted hell; the last of the eight great hot hells, whose sufferers die and are reborn incessantly.

bhikshu   Literally, "beggar." A religious mendicant who has left home and renounced all possessions in order to follow the Way of the Buddha and who has become a fully ordained monk.

bhikshuni   A Buddhist nun observing the same rules as a *bhikshu*.

bodhisattva   *Bodhi*, buddhahood; *sattva*, living being. (1) A being in the final stage prior to attaining buddhahood. (2) One who devotes himself to attaining enlightenment not only for himself but also for all sentient beings.

Bodhi tree   The name of the tree under which Shakyamuni was seated in meditation when he attained enlightenment.

Brahma deities   The gods of Hinduism. In Buddhism, the chief of them, Brahma, is the lord of the world of form.

buddha   A title meaning "one who is enlightened," or "enlightened one." With a capital and a preceding "the," it means Shakyamuni. Buddhas are those who have completely realized the truth of all things in the universe.

buddha-nature   The potential for attaining buddhahood, or potential for enlightenment, innate in every sentient being.

cause and effect   *See* law of cause and effect.

Chih-i   Chinese patriarch (538–97) of the T'ien-t'ai (Japanese, Tendai) sect.

circle of white hair between eyebrows   One of the thirty-two signs of excellence of face and figure of the Buddha. The symbol of complete wisdom. *See* thirty-two signs.

dharani   Literally, "wholly grasping." A magic spell or incantation. In the Lotus Sutra, *dharanis* are offered to safeguard the sutra and its followers.

Eightfold Path   Right view, right thinking, right speech, right action, right living, right endeavor, right memory, right meditation. The teaching that shows the right way to live our daily lives.

Eternal Original Buddha   The absolute, omnipresent existence that always causes all things to live. The Eternal Original Buddha has been and will be teaching, leading, and benefiting all sentient beings from the infinite past to the infinite future.

faith and discernment   Faith is the working of one's emotions; discernment is the working of one's reason. Unless a religion combines both of them, it does not have true power.

five categories   (1) Rejoicing over the Lotus Sutra, (2) reading and reciting it, (3) preaching it to others, (4) concurrently practicing the Six Perfections of a bodhisattva, and (5) fully practicing the Six Perfections.

five practices of teachers of the Law   (1) Receiving and keeping the Lotus Sutra, (2) reading it, (3) reciting it, (4) expounding it, and (5) copying it.

four faiths   (1) Receiving but one thought of faith and discernment concerning the eternity of the Buddha's life, (2) apprehending its meaning, (3) devoting oneself to preaching the Lotus Sutra to others, and (4) perfecting profound faith and discernment.

four groups   The four classes of the Buddha's disciples:

bhikshus (monks), *bhikshunis* (nuns), *upasakas* (male lay believers), and *upasikas* (female lay believers).

Four Noble Truths (1) All existence entails suffering (the Truth of Suffering). (2) Suffering is caused by ignorance, which gives rise to craving and illusion (the Truth of Cause). (3) There is an end to suffering, and this state of no suffering is called nirvana (the Truth of Extinction). (4) Nirvana is attained through the practice of the Eightfold Path and the Six Perfections (the Truth of the Path).

innumerable meanings The term has two senses: (1) the real aspect of all things, of all forms in the universe—the true form at the heart of the apparent world visible to the eye—and (2) the countless phenomena of the visible world brought forth from the one true world that is the real aspect of all things.

karma Originally, "deed." It often means the results of deeds, which may be either good or bad. All that one is at the present moment is the result of karma that he has produced in the past.

Law The truth; the teaching of the Buddha.

Law-body of the Buddha The ultimate substance or entity of the Buddha not apparent to the eye.

Law-Flower Sutra Another name for the Sutra of the Lotus Flower of the Wonderful Law.

Law of Appearance The teaching based on the wisdom of the Buddha appearing in history—that is, Shakyamuni. The Law of Appearance teaches that the final purpose of human beings is to attain the state of buddhahood.

Law of Causation The central doctrine of Buddhism, which teaches that all phenomena result from the combination of causes and conditions. According to this doctrine, all things in the universe exist in interrelationship with one another ("Nothing has an ego"), and all things and phenomena in this world constantly change ("All things are impermanent").

law of cause and effect   Normally considered as part of the Law of Causation, the law of cause and effect treats of the Law of Causation as it relates to an individual.

Law of Origin   The teaching expressing the salvation of man through the Original Buddha's compassion.

Law of the Twelve Causes   This law teaches that all phenomena in this world constantly change and that all changes are based on an established rule divided into twelve stages: (1) ignorance, (2) actions, (3) consciousness, (4) name and form (mental functions and matter), (5) the six entrances (the five senses and the mind), (6) contact, (7) sensation, (8) desire, (9) clinging, (10) existence, (11) birth, and (12) old age and death. According to this doctrine, the fundamental cause of all human suffering is ignorance.

Mahayana   Literally, "great vehicle." One of the two major divisions of Buddhism, together with the Theravada (Hinayana) school. The more liberal and practical of the two major schools, with its scriptures written in Sanskrit.

Maitreya   "The Friendly One." One of the three important bodhisattvas who embody the virtues of the Buddha. Manjushri ("The Beautiful Auspicious One") embodies the Buddha's wisdom; Maitreya, his compassion; Universal Virtue, his practice.

Manjushri   *See* Maitreya.

mappo   The period of the Decay of the Law; the corrupt age.

merit   Generally, the change for the better in life that one gains through the change in his mental state by believing in and practicing a correct religion. Divided roughly into the mental or spiritual kind and the physical or material kind.

Namah   Literally, "bend, incline, bow, submit." Often

translated as "I pay homage to," "I submit myself to," or "I take refuge in," as in "*Namah* Shakyamuni Buddha."

Nichiren   Japanese Buddhist priest (1222–82) and founder of the Nichiren sect.

nirvana   Literally, "extinction." The state of peace and quietude that is attained by extinguishing all illusions; the death of the Buddha.

One Buddha-vehicle   The concept that the three vehicles (*shravaka, pratyekabuddha,* and bodhisattva) are as such one.

Original Buddha   The Buddha who exists in every part of the universe from the infinite past to the infinite future.

pratyekabuddha   One who attains personal enlightenment through his own independent practice, without a teacher.

prediction   The assurance given by the Buddha that one will certainly become a buddha in the future after long practice.

real aspect   The fundamental nondifferentiation at the heart of things is the one law that calls all things into being and moves them. This is called the real aspect of things.

saha-world   The world of suffering; this world.

sangha   The monastic community of Buddhist monks or nuns; more generally, the community of Buddhist believers.

seven parables of the Lotus Sutra   (1) The parable of the burning house; (2) the parable of the poor son; (3) the parable of the herbs; (4) the parable of the city in a vision; (5) the parable of the gem in the robe; (6) the parable of the gem in the topknot; (7) the parable of the physician's sons.

Shakyamuni   Literally, "sage of the Shakyas" (the tribe from which the Buddha came). The usual Mahayana Buddhist appellation of the historical Buddha (c. 560 to c. 480 B.C.).

shravaka   Literally, "one who hears"—that is, who hears the voice of the Buddha and thereby reaches personal enlightenment.

Six Perfections   The six kinds of practice that bodhisattvas should follow to attain enlightenment. This doctrine has the salvation of all living beings as its aim. The Six Perfections are (1) donation, (2) keeping the precepts, (3) perseverance, (4) assiduity, (5) meditation, and (6) wisdom.

stupa   A pagoda or dagoba in which sacred relics are deposited. Originally a tomb, then a cenotaph, it is now for the most part merely a symbol of Buddhism.

sutra   Literally, "thread" or "string." A scripture containing the teachings of the Buddha.

tactfulness or tactful way   The Buddha's wise method of leading people to the attainment of buddhahood.

tathagata   Literally, "one who has come of truth"—that is, one who has come from the truth to show it to the world. It is the highest epithet of a buddha.

ten merits   The merits one can gain from understanding of the teachings in the Sutra of Innumerable Meanings. These are stated in chapter 3 of the sutra.

Ten Suchnesses   The doctrine that all existence has (1) such a form, (2) such a nature, (3) such an embodiment, (4) such a potency, (5) such a function, (6) such a primary cause, (7) such a secondary cause, (8) such an effect, (9) such a recompense, and (10) such a complete fundamental whole. The spirit of the Lotus Sutra is philosophically condensed into this doctrine.

thirty-two signs of excellence of face and figure   The auspicious marks and characteristics that a buddha has on his body. He acquires them as a result of his practicing good deeds as a bodhisattva for an extremely long period.

three-thousand-great-thousandfold world   The chiliocosm. According to ancient Indian cosmology, the universe consists of an infinite number of worlds, all more or less on the same plan as our own. The term thus suggests infinity.

Three Thousand Realms in One Mind   This doctrine teaches that we have the infinite possibility of moving both upward and downward and that if we resolve firmly to practice the Buddha's teachings, we can go upward without fail.

Twelve Causes   *See* Law of the Twelve Causes.

Universal Virtue   *See* Maitreya

upasaka   A male lay believer in Buddhism.

upasika   A female lay believer in Buddhism.

void   The undifferentiated absolute. The meaning is not "nothingness" but "equality": the idea that all things, including matter, the human mind, and events originate from the same foundation.

Vulture Peak   A mountain near present-day Rajgir, Bihar, in northeastern India. Its name is said to derive from the fact that its peak is shaped like a vulture and also that many vultures are supposed to have lived on the mountain.

Way   The true and correct path toward enlightenment and buddhahood.

World-honored One   An epithet of a buddha and of Shakyamuni.

Index